# Do These Jeans Make Me Look Fat?

## Breaking the Cultural Mirror

Published by Barbour Publishing, Inc., P.O. Box 719, Uhrichsville, Ohio 44683,
www.barbourbooks.com

*Our mission is to publish and distribute inspirational products offering exceptional
value and biblical encouragement to the masses.*

 Member of the
Evangelical Christian
Publishers Association

Printed in the United States of America.

# Do These Jeans Make Me Look Fat?

## Breaking the Cultural Mirror

Jocelyn Hamsher

BARBOUR
PUBLISHING

## Dedication

This book is dedicated to women everywhere,
and especially to those who come after. My nieces—
Abby, Carrie, Brittany, Roxanne, Katie, Emma, Brooke,
and Faith—you have just been handed the bigger picture.
You, my precious ones, are absolutely beautiful.

# Thank-Yous

Jesus, thank You that because of You, there is a bigger picture to pass along. I am forever grateful. Words cannot express all that You have done and how You have loved me. This message is Yours—do with it what only You can. We want to walk in the desires of Your heart.

Bruce, the love of my life, thank you for being my biggest encourager and support. Thank you for your heart of wisdom and for loving me beautifully. It is a privilege living God's adventure with you. I love you and thank you for who you are and all that you give. God gifted me above and beyond.

Micah, Ty, and Cade, my precious sons, you treat me like a queen. I love you like a crazy woman and the way God made each of you. Thank you for making our family that much better. I am one blessed momma to have you guys.

Denise, thank you for the work you put into this project. You not only have added fun to this book but you have added fun to my life. You are truly one of God's delights.

Thank you to the many women who have contributed to this book. You have shared not only your stories and perspectives but also life lessons. It is a privilege to learn from you.

Thank you to the prayer warriors who have covered me and the writing of this book. Thank you for your time, heart, and passion in approaching the throne of grace. Your prayers are powerful and invaluable. As always, Jesus is faithful to do what He promises.

Janine, Elizabeth, and Rachele, my dear sisters, thank you for your work in this project through editing, prayers, and encouragement. Your friendship is priceless.

Lisa, Missy, Dawn, Dayna, and Beth—thank you for being vessels of God's grace and blessings not only to me but to many. Thank you to my circle of friends—all those women in my life who influence me and grow me up. It is a privilege to do life with you and serve our King together. I love you dearly.

A special thank-you to Kelly McIntosh, Mary Burns, Lora Schrock, Kelsey Keller, and the rest of the Barbour team for all your hard work and help in this project.

# Contents

# Introduction

My husband and I had taken our sons to the friendly, but ever-so-crowded water park for the day. Despite the noise and multitude of kids swimming under and around us like fish, we leisurely floated down the "lazy river" on our inner tube, basking in the sun. Every now and then a mechanically forced current from the side of the river would propel us along. I remember thinking that with as many people as there were, we had miraculously steered clear of taking anyone "out" along the way. My thoughts were premature. As the jet-propelled current kicked into full force, it managed to catapult us forward. And, with our legs hanging out over the front of the tube, it happened. The picture was surreal and seemingly in slow motion. I saw her black-suited backside and my husband's foot headed right toward it. In a heroic attempt to prevent either of them from any humiliation, his leg and foot recoiled, toes even curled as to avoid this collision at all costs. His chivalrous act failed. And just as quickly as we had come, we were gone. No words were exchanged or apology extended, for we never saw her face. She never turned around.

As we "bounced" off and continued floating down-river, my head was no longer upright. It was resting on the back of the tube and my body convulsing with laughter. I replayed the event over in my mind, watched as my husband tried to escape on the tube as quickly as possible, and now witnessed his quiet smile and shaking head. It was all just plain hilarious. Knowing my husband as the storyteller he is, I knew this one was going to be one of his trophies. Don't get me wrong—I felt for that lady. In fact, I was mortified for her. I could put myself in her shoes in an instant. How many times have situations concerning our bodies, through no fault of our own, made us paranoid, self-focused, and even confirmed our discontentedness? How many times have we gone to the pool or even the gym, took one look around and felt immediately dissatisfied with ourselves? How many times have we worked tirelessly to change the things we can and have grown despairing over the things we can't? The way we see ourselves affects the way we see our world. So it's time to broaden our perspective.

I am getting older and even though I can't say that I wrestle anymore with my body not being the perfect "ten" (I guess nowadays society would say the perfect "four"), I definitely am experiencing the changes that life and gravity bring. No matter where we stand emotionally or physically on the body image spectrum, it is a topic that is relevant for all of us to talk about, so we want to do just that in the following pages. My prayer is that by the end of this book you will see your body through a different lens, with more value, significance, and honor than you ever realized your body held. May it transform the way you see God, others, the world around you, and yourself. May it transform the way you live life. Be blessed and enjoy!

## Chapter 1

# DO THESE JEANS MAKE ME LOOK FAT?

Don't become so well-adjusted to
your culture that you fit into it
without even thinking.
Instead, fix your attention on God.
You'll be changed from the inside out. . . .
Unlike the culture around you,
always dragging you down to its
level of immaturity, God brings the
best out of you, develops
well-formed maturity in you.

ROMANS 12:2 MSG

# Praise for
## *Do These Jeans Make Me Look Fat?*

"I love this book, and I love this gal! Jocelyn Hamsher is a new voice for women who want to run the race of faith with honesty, humor, and honor. Wish I'd had this decades ago!"
—Virelle Kidder, conference speaker and author of *Meet Me at the Well* and *The Best Life Ain't Easy*

"Writing with warmth and humor, Jocelyn communicates God's love, grace, and truth on an issue that is too often a source of frustration and even self-contempt for women. This book makes an important contribution for any woman who is struggling to accept and make peace with her body."
—Janice Hershberger, professional clinical counselor

"Jocelyn Hamsher has scored a hit with her new book, *Do These Jeans Make Me Look Fat?* . . . She speaks wisdom, encouragement, and great hope into the soul of every woman (no matter her age) who is willing to embrace her very wise words. May you read this authentic, practical work with great joy."
—Jan Silvious, author of *Same Life, New Story*

"*Do These Jeans Make Me Look Fat? Breaking the Cultural Mirror* is a must-read for women of all ages. Jocelyn Hamsher takes a look into this serious subject with hilarious stories and a realness that is refreshing. As a survivor of an eating disorder, I find this book

quite helpful and real. As someone who now loves her "culturally imperfect" body, I think this book will help women of all ages to move towards loving their bodies and appreciating the miracles our bodies truly are."
—Wilma Mast, pastor and clinical counselor

"In *Do These Jeans Make Me Look Fat?—Breaking the Cultural Mirror* I hear the humor, the biblical scholarship, and heart that *is* Jocelyn Hamsher. A quick and delightful read, this book should be in the tool belt of every parent and mentor that has opportunity to invest in the lives of women. . . . This book simply expands her existing ministry of in-depth teaching, speaking, and encouragement that Jocelyn is so well known for. . . ."
—Lisa Troyer, Circle of Friends Ministries

"Jocelyn Hamsher captures the heart of every woman in *Do These Jeans Make Me Look Fat?* We wish we were spiritual enough to quit focusing on our body image and embrace the One who loves us just the way we are, but it's hard to break the mold of self-criticism when our culture demands perfection. Jocelyn skillfully reminds us to see ourselves through the mirror of God's Word. I highly recommend this book for personal and small group study."
—Carol Kent, speaker and author of *Between a Rock and a Grace Place*

> The woman wins who calls herself beautiful and challenges the world to change to truly see her.
>
> NAOMI WOLF

Every single woman has done it. The compulsive slow turn in front of the mirror, neck cranked to 180 degrees, voicing the automatic question linked to that pose: "Do these jeans make me look fat?" Or even better, "Do these jeans make my butt look big?" Whether the question is thought silently or vocalized to some poor unsuspecting victim in the room, it is a question every woman has stared down. However "natural" and seemingly harmless that question appears to be, what does asking it evoke in us? When we walked out of the house that morning, how did it taint our feelings, thoughts, and perspectives about ourselves, our relationships, our value, and our purpose?

Let's say you have met a wonderful man who has become your best friend, you dated him for some time and then decided to marry. The wedding was absolutely

beautiful, all your friends and family were present making the day even more meaningful, and the reception was a great celebration. Put simply, it was the most memorable day of your life. You can hardly wait to see the pictures to relive it once again. The day arrives, and you rush to the photographer's to pick up the proofs. Smiling, she hands you the portfolio, and as you open it, your face falls and horror seizes your heart. Every single picture displays only half of what it should. Half of people's faces are cut off, half of the wedding cake is missing, half of the bridal party is gone, and from the way the picture turned out, it will remain a mystery who it is you were kissing to seal the deal. No matter how beautiful the wedding was, you can't see it in its entirety because you only have half the picture. And so it is with our bodies. We are walking around looking in mirrors without seeing the entire, true, and beautiful picture.

In order to see this larger, truer picture, this chapter is devoted to painting and acknowledging the picture we are already gazing on and believing is the whole. In other words, it's time to recognize the lies our culture is speaking about our bodies—their purpose, their appearance, and their value—and how such lies are affecting all those believing them, including you and me. They are reflected in how we think, what we say, what we choose, and how we behave. You don't have to look very far to see or hear the impact, because up to eight out of ten women struggle with body dissatisfaction.[1] I saw some very open, honest,

---

1. Linda S. Mintle, "Making Peace with Your Thighs," *Christian Counseling Today* 13, no. 4 (2005).

and valid questions the other day posted online by one young woman: "Thinking about us women this morning and the pressures we put on ourselves. Does there ever come a time that we completely accept ourselves? The good, the bad, the ugly, the cellulite. Do we ever gain victory over the enemy's attack and see ourselves as the beautiful women God made us? Is it a constant battle we continually need God's help to fight?" As others read her questions and responded, one response in particular caught my attention: "Just being content doesn't seem popular! Why do we strive to be better than other people or strive to be the best?"

Being content doesn't seem popular. I would agree wholeheartedly. We do strive to be better than others, or at least as good as others, don't we? I had a young woman tell me the other day that she would rather have people tell her she is too skinny than have them tell her she looks great. I was perplexed by her statement until she explained. With their seemingly negative "too skinny" comment, comes extra attention—attention she desires. And in her mind, she stands out to the crowd. She's noticed, she's special, she's significant. And she's not alone. Our battle with body image. . .I would say something deeper is going on.

Misguided attitudes and beliefs not only affect women in the States but also worldwide. In 2003, a total of 45,000 European women were polled regarding their body image. Over half (60 percent) said they could not stand the way they looked, while only a mere 4 percent

of women said they were "completely happy." Over half of the total women polled said they would change one or two things with cosmetic surgery if it were free, and 40 percent confessed they worry about their body shape every day.[2] These statistics beg us to ask some very real questions of ourselves, and it's okay to be transparent. In fact, we need to be. Why the poor view of our bodies? Why the obsession? Why the neglect? What is the reason for our discontentedness? Are we truly unhealthy and need to do things differently? Whose standard are we using to define ourselves? Is it possible to obtain a real and lasting peace about our bodies, about who we are, about who we are becoming? And not only a peace, but a joy as well?

To continue to see the picture we hold in our hand, we need to understand that we are looking at an even more heart-wrenching and alarming situation. We as adult women aren't the only ones affected by the lies. The precious younger ones following us are exposed and succumbing to them as well. Working as a registered nurse in a family practice office, I clearly remember weighing a ten-year-old girl. As she stepped off the scale, she ran from the room in tears. Encouraging her to express her feelings, she proceeded to tell me she needed to lose weight—she was just too fat. I want to clarify that this ten-year-old was not overweight but exhibited a healthy profile for her age and height. She's not alone. By the age of ten, 81 percent of girls are afraid of being

---

2. "Most Women 'Hate Their Bodies,'" BBC, accessed October 20, 2003, http://bbc.co.uk/2hi/uk-news/32-6236.stm.

fat.[3] Girls as young as six are dissatisfied with their bodies. In fact, 40 percent of girls ages six through twelve already want to change their appearance. They compare themselves to their Barbie dolls or even to one of their favorite shows, *America's Next Top Model.* Complaints are comprised of big bottoms or thighs and stomachs that aren't flat enough. One twelve-year-old already has a dream of cosmetic surgery to enhance her bustline. The article concludes that children don't seem to be allowed to be kids anymore. In fact, society seems to be teaching little girls to be their own worst critic.[4]

When I talked with several women about their own body image, it was interesting to discover that their awareness of how they looked, especially to others, began with someone's negative comment in their early years. They cited examples of others who were critical of their appearance, from what they were wearing to their body type, singling them out and making them feel unacceptable and ugly. Whether it be a parent or peer, whether well intentioned or not, the words we speak have meaning. It is sobering how powerful words can be, especially at a young age. But something that made me stop in my tracks was the thought of the indirect messages we convey, perhaps not what these young ones are hearing, but what they are catching. Are we negative about how *we* look? Are *we* never satisfied or critical of

3. Linda S. Mintle, "Making Peace with Your Thighs," *Christian Counseling Today* 13, no. 4 (2005).
4. Alison Smith-Squire, "Girls as Young as SIX Who Already Hate Their Bodies," *Mail*, December 7, 2007, http://www.dailymail.co.uk/The-Girls-young-SIX-hate-bodies.html.

ourselves or others? Do *we* obsess over our bodies in one extreme or another? Do *we* neglect or abuse our bodies—perhaps shown through apathy or bad habits we have adopted?

Fortunately our messages can impact positively as well. One evening as one of my dear friends rocked her five-year-old daughter, they shared back and forth about "life." She asked her daughter as she snuggled in her arms, "Do you think that you will still let me hold you like this when you're all grown up?" Her little girl looked up at her mother in all seriousness and responded, "When I'm all grown up I want to have red glasses, wear Grandma's jewelry, and have big boobs. . ."—all descriptions of her precious momma. The way we carry ourselves, our beliefs, attitudes, and perceptions of our bodies, of our very lives, are all caught by those watching. Will they be positive or negative? Will they be steeped in truth or lies? Will it be the whole picture or a facade of one? We are passing on something—what is it?

As my friend walked alongside the pool where her kids were swimming, her seven-year-old daughter yelled out, "Hey Mom, you have life preservers in your swimsuit!" My friend looked at her, confused, and asked "What?" Her daughter yelled again matter-of-factly, "You have life preservers in your suit!" My friend glanced over her shoulder and said, "No, I don't, that's my rear end!" Jumping out of the pool, her daughter ran up to her and poked her finger into my friend's backside needing to prove it to herself: "Oh yeah, it *is* your butt."

And with a carefree spirit, she turned and jumped back into the pool. I love this story because it was spoken in absolute innocence and it is hilarious. How many of us can see ourselves in this mother's shoes? But it brings up another question that may make us shift in our seat. How are we looking at others? Rather than seeing others as He made them to be, and encouraging them in that identity, we have a tendency to look at their appearance and view them through the eyes of the world. We have all done it, perhaps not meaning to, but with a word or a look have we reinforced the world's standard of defining a person's worth?

I had the privilege of asking family practitioner Dr. Eric Miller about some of the issues he runs into in his office on a regular basis, specifically asking about the attitudes and beliefs he sees in women and girls related to our culture's philosophies. One of the points he made would be an eye-opening one for many. I asked, "Culture has placed such a high emphasis on being thin. But thin doesn't necessarily mean healthy, correct?" I really enjoyed his response:

*"It is better to be fat and fit, than thin and out of shape. Statistics show us that the overweight woman that can jog a few miles lives longer than the thin one that doesn't exercise. Even the overweight person who is in good cardiovascular shape is less likely to have events like the biggest killer in the US—heart attacks. Ideally, of course,*

*we would be both thin and fit. But remember to look at the big picture of health and realize that it is not just about being thin. It is about being healthy. This is the biggest lie I see women buying into—we say we want to be thin and fit so that we will remain healthy, but we really want to be thin so that we look good. This perversion is taught to us at an early age, especially to girls. So we end up using unhealthy ways—fad diets that don't work or even smoking—to try and stay looking healthy rather than truly being healthy."*

This is radically countercultural to today's thinking and standard. For so long, we have focused on outward appearance and neglected the condition within, physically and emotionally—in ourselves and in others.

Michelle Graham, author and speaker, shares about the world's perspective of beauty in the form of Barbie. Bless Barbie's heart, but she would have some serious physical problems if she ever graced reality. You may have heard this before, but it is worth the repeat. Graham says that if Barbie actually were a human, she'd have a bust of thirty-six inches, and her proportions would make her well over six feet tall. To achieve her hourglass figure, she'd have to have several organs removed. And the gap between her thighs? It could be the result of a major bone deformity.[5]

We have heard of the impressive technology that uses

---

5. Michelle Graham, *Wanting to Be Her: Body Image Secrets Victoria Won't Tell You* (Downers Grove, IL: InterVarsity Press, 2005), 12–13.

airbrushing and electronic altering to make photographs of models appear flawless. Our culture has set perfection as the standard in order to be accepted as beautiful. Because of that lie, we continue to kill ourselves to try to reach something that is impossible this side of heaven. Graham shares that in the past thirty years, most Miss America winners have sported a body mass index within the range of malnutrition. The majority (75 percent) of the female characters in TV sitcoms are underweight. Only one celebrity out of twenty is average in size.[6] These statistics pull back the curtain and reveal the facade we have been buying into. God gave us each a body type, and what's happening is that we are attempting to make our bodies something they were never meant to be, something we can't sustain and be healthy. Only 5 percent of women have a tiny frame, which has been the prototype of the supermodel.[7] We are attempting to be someone else and missing out on who God made us to be. My heart breaks for the generations coming behind us that are falling into the trap. Teenage girls who have a beautiful future and incredible potential are viewing commercials depicting women who model the unrealistically thin, "ideal" type of beauty, and they are feeling angrier, less confident, and more dissatisfied with their weight and appearance.[8]

Several years ago, I had the privilege of mentoring a beautiful young woman who was recovering from an

6. Linda S. Mintle, "Making Peace with Your Thighs," *Christian Counseling Today* 13, no. 4 (2005).

7. Ibid.

8. Ibid.

eating disorder. Monica's concern over her weight had begun in seventh grade and hit rock bottom in high school. She says her routine was to eat, laugh, pretend that everything was normal, then run to the bathroom to purge. Her physical behavior was simply the reflection of her beliefs and thoughts. In one of her school reports, "Dying to Be Beautiful," she describes what she had learned through her experience:

> The fact that needs to be recognized is what an eating disorder does to its quarry's mind, body, and spirit and just how much destruction an eating disorder wreaks on its victim. Living within the grip of disordered eating is like a person's worst nightmare coming alive, times four. In the beginning a person feels like they have the control, but slowly the eating disorder begins to usurp their life, eating away their mind, their spirit, and their body, one pound at a time. However, it doesn't stop there; this demon is not satisfied until it has completely ravaged its prey, leaving the person only a shadow of what they once were, or even worse, dead. Yes, dead, gone, already a skeleton before they are buried, our average Janes are dying to be beautiful. In fact, statistics show that in one person's lifetime 50,000 people die from an eating disorder. Women, is that understood? We are dying, because we have chosen to believe lies.

Granted, not every woman succumbs to an eating disorder, but the point is that the thoughts and beliefs that our culture is producing are toxic. No matter who we try to blame—whether it be messages through television, billboards, others' opinions and perspectives, or hurtful comments spoken in childhood—we who live in this culture need to learn not only how to deal with these messages but also how to overcome the lies enmeshed within them. As my husband says, "You either stop the sin or the sin stops you." In this case, we either stop the lies, or they will stop us.

So how do we do that? Romans 12:2 (MSG) cautions "Don't become so well-adjusted to your culture that you fit into it without even thinking. Instead, fix your attention on God. You'll be changed from the inside out." The New International Version phrases it, "Do not conform to the pattern of this world, but be transformed by the renewing of your mind." The world is obviously thinking one way, and we have seen the results. Unfortunately, we have been found guilty of buying into it more often than not. In an article by Laura Fraser, she reports that women have a mental picture of themselves that doesn't fit their actual size. We have heard that those who suffer from anorexia can look in the mirror and see excess body fat. Fraser reports that psychologists who have studied the anorexic's response have compared it to the responses of "normal" women. It turns out that the average woman also views herself as much larger than she really is! When psychologists at St. George's Hospital Medical School in

London asked fifty normal-sized women to estimate the width of a box, they were quite accurate. But when asked to estimate their body widths, they exaggerated their size. The only ones happy with their size were ten pounds underweight.[9]

We have a vision problem. We have been looking back and forth at others rather than looking up. We also have a heart problem—we haven't believed the truth. From my experience and that of the countless others I've talked to, obsession with body image is just one more trap Satan uses to keep us squelched and distracted from walking as the person God has made us to be. Satan has used our preoccupation with how we look to deceive us from discovering what our bodies are truly about and what they were intended for.

It's time to begin thinking and believing in a new and true way, and we find that way in God's Word. The Bible tells us we can be transformed, experiencing a new nature by renewing our minds with truth. Much like a caterpillar metamorphosing into a butterfly, our thoughts, our perspectives, our vision, and behavior can be changed from an old way of thinking, perceiving, and behaving to a new way. It is a way that leads us into peace, joy, and freedom. So, how do we stop the lies? By continuing to identify the lies as they pummel us, while learning the truth found in God's Word. With each lie identified, we replace it with truth because it is the truth that will set

9. Laura Fraser, "Women: Building a Better Body Image," A Healthy Me, http://www.ahealthyme.com/topic/bodyimagewomen.

us free (see John 8:32). It is a process, one that doesn't occur overnight. And Satan, knowing it is a struggle, can continue to taunt us in those areas, but as we live out the truth and choose to believe it, the power and life found in Jesus and in God's Word begins to transform us.

How do we stop the lies? It is one thing to know truth, but it is another to walk in it. A young lady shared with me that no matter how many times she hears that she doesn't need the approval of society, she confesses she still wants it. She's being honest, and one can't fault her for that. And when we begin to walk more consistently in truth, we will then begin to experience more and more of who God made us to be. The difference between knowing and growing is obedience. So as we learn truth, we are faced with the choice of choosing it moment by moment. Will we choose to stop viewing our bodies with narcissistic eyes and begin viewing them through another lens—God's lens, the One who made us, the One who knew us before time began? In my husband's book, *Bouquets: Intentional Relationships in Making Disciples*, Bruce shares this general thought: If you had a troubleshooting question about your computer, who would you want to ask—the one who sold it to you or the one who designed it? If you had any doubts about the strength of the bridge you were about to cross, who would you feel better asking, the guy driving the car in front of you or the engineer? If you were seeking to understand the inspiration behind a painting, would you want to ask the tour guide or the artist himself? So why would we not go to the One who fashioned and created us to discover the truth about His creation, His prized possession?[10] What if we made our bodies less about us and more about Jesus? How would these actions affect our world? How would these choices naturally affect the way we care for our bodies? Would our preoccupation with our bodies disappear if our hearts changed along with our gaze? *Fix your attention on God and you'll be changed.*

Our battle with body image goes deeper than what we know. And the thrilling and freeing truth is that we can go that deep with Him, learning and discovering things hidden in our hearts, and He won't leave us or let us go. He will, in fact, love us all the way through and bring a new perspective, a renewed relationship based in perfect love and joy. In the following chapters, we are going to leap into the truth of God's Word, laugh as we resonate with other women's stories, learn as we are challenged to think bigger, and listen for God's voice as He speaks to each one of us about our bodies and about our relationship with Him. Culture's foundation of beauty is fallible because it's built on lies. It's time for us to arm ourselves with truth and expose the lies brewing in our minds and taking root in our hearts. It's time to choose and believe what God says, walk in the freedom of who He made us to be, and discover how beautiful our bodies truly are. Whether you know it or not, you are a woman

---

10. Bruce Hamsher, *Bouquets: Intentional Relationships in Making Disciples* (Scottdale, PA: Herald Press, 2008). Used by permission.

of influence to somebody, if not to many. No matter how old you are, you have been given this gift. You may have a daughter, granddaughter, niece, friend, mother, sister, neighbor, coworker, team member, or someone else in your sphere of influence that needs to have the blinders removed from her eyes and be encouraged, taught, and loved with truth. We have a wonderful opportunity and yes, a responsibility, to learn, live out, and speak truth to the women all around us, and to the generations who come after us. We are all holding one of two possible pictures in our hearts and minds that we depict as real. One is complete, the other is not. Which picture will we pass on?

# DISCUSSION QUESTIONS

1. Have you ever struck the infamous pose in front of the mirror? How did what you see taint how you felt about yourself?

2. What is your perspective regarding your body image? What do you want to look like? What do you want to hear from people? Now explain why. Is there something deeper going on?

3. Looking around, where or how have you witnessed culture's lies regarding the definition of beauty?

4. How have you impacted others around you in regard to body image? What has been said or implied? Has it been positive or negative?

5. Discuss your response to Dr. Miller's statement on page 23. How has this impacted you?

6. How have you viewed others who don't fit into society's standard? Have you viewed them through your eyes or God's?

7. Just from reading chapter one, what lies were exposed that you have believed about your body or yourself?

8. How much of your perspective regarding your body has been about God?

9. Write Romans 12:2 on an index card and place it in a spot where you will see it every day. How can you apply this verse in your life?

# Notes

........................................................

........................................................

........................................................

........................................................

........................................................

........................................................

........................................................

........................................................

........................................................

........................................................

........................................................

........................................................

........................................................

........................................................

........................................................

........................................................

# Notes

........................................................

........................................................

........................................................

........................................................

........................................................

........................................................

........................................................

........................................................

........................................................

........................................................

........................................................

........................................................

........................................................

........................................................

........................................................

# Notes

........................................................................

........................................................................

........................................................................

........................................................................

........................................................................

........................................................................

........................................................................

........................................................................

........................................................................

........................................................................

........................................................................

........................................................................

........................................................................

........................................................................

# Notes

# Notes

........................................................................

........................................................................

........................................................................

........................................................................

........................................................................

........................................................................

........................................................................

........................................................................

........................................................................

........................................................................

........................................................................

........................................................................

........................................................................

........................................................................

*Chapter 2*

## DUCT TAPE, UNDERWIRE, AND OTHER TRANSFORMING THOUGHTS

For in him all things were created:
things in heaven and on earth,
visible and invisible,
whether thrones or powers or rulers
or authorities; all things have been
created through him and for him.

COLOSSIANS 1:16 NIV

> Men go abroad to wonder at the height
> of mountains, at the huge waves of the
> sea, at the long courses of the rivers,
> at the vast compass of the ocean,
> at the circular motion of the stars;
> and they pass by themselves
> without wondering.
>
> SAINT AUGUSTINE

A friend of mine was getting ready to attend an evening event when she realized the shirt she was wearing was overemphasizing what she has termed her "back fat." After trying on the binder she wore after the birth of her children and discovering it was too big, she went for something much more practical. With multiple kids my friend has had to get creative, and duct tape has been the answer for a multitude of queries. From doors to diapers, duct tape has proved tried and true. So, it was no different in her mind as she raced out the door, binder on the floor and duct tape in hand. As her husband drove to their engagement (all the while shaking his head), she and her daughters sat in the backseat painstakingly wrapping her torso in duct tape. (If you ever want to try this, she describes the experience as hot and very uncomfortable but highly effective in a pinch.) Despite the fact that she couldn't bend over and knew if anyone hugged her she would become their evening's mystery, she says it was worth the adventure. Fortunately, when removing the duct tape her skin was unscathed because of the short duration the tape had been worn (so if you try this at home, be mindful of this crucial variable). I never found out about her secret until she tried it a second time when I was with her at a friend's house, and she managed to bend over, revealing the tape. Apparently, it was a trick that worked for her successfully enough that it was worth the repeat.

Haven't we all tried to cover up, minimize, or disguise our imperfections to make ourselves look and feel better? You bet. If we want to minimize, we will pull on our girdles, control-top tights, or anything that will suck us in. If we want to feel enhanced, we will grab the underwire, padded, or push-up bra—whatever it takes to transform us. In chapter one, we established the fact that our vision has been skewed for various reasons. Now, it's time to look at the entire picture. So while you are reading this chapter, I want you to stop looking at yourself. I want you to stop looking at others. During this chapter, I want you to look up. Only up, so we can begin to discover the tool of transformation that really works. I am asking that you open your heart and mind to the words of God about your body. We are not talking about your body's appearance right now, but how sacred and valuable it truly is. We are talking about its purpose, its dignity, and the high calling of what it was made to do and who it was made for. That alone makes your body absolutely beautiful. Whether you are a believer or not, you must know that your body was made by God, the Creator of all things. Colossians 1:16 (NIV) says, "For in him [Jesus] all things were created: things in heaven and on earth, visible and invisible, whether thrones or powers or rulers or authorities; all things have been created through and for him." The One who knows each star by name and hung the moon, who set limits to the seas and every morning gives the sun orders to rise, who raises His voice to the clouds sending rain and lightning bolts on their way—this same God created you. And guess what? You take dibs. Out of all the beautiful things God created, He called you His prize creation. This is what David wrote, but read it as if you did:

*Oh yes, you shaped me first inside, then out;
you formed me in my mother's womb. I thank
you, High God—you're breathtaking! Body
and soul, I am marvelously made! I worship in
adoration—what a creation! You know me inside
and out, you know every bone in my body; you
know exactly how I was made, bit by bit, how*

*I was sculpted from nothing into something.*
*Like an open book, you watched me grow from*
*conception to birth; all the stages of my life were*
*spread out before you, the days of my life all*
*prepared before I'd even lived one day.* PSALM
*139:13–16 (MSG)*

Your body has been made in a miraculous way.
We could make a long list about the incredible, mind-
blowing things God wired your body to do, but start
with these: Did you know your eyes take in more
information than the largest telescope known to man[11]
and are so intricately crafted they can distinguish 500
shades of gray?[12] Your nose can discern 50,000 scents
without effort.[13] Each cell in your body (all 100 trillion)
is a tiny factory that mirrors a high-tech industrialized
city, working for the body to repair damage, manufacture
and transport energy, communicate with other cells,
and protect the body. Each microscopic cell holds DNA
(a genetic code or "blueprint" that is responsible for
every characteristic of a person), which is six to eight
feet long.[14] I could point out that your brain is more
complex than the most powerful computer, possessing
an inconceivable 100 billion nerve cells. And guess what?
Just one of those cells has the capacity to hold as much

---

11. "Amazing Human Facts," Hub Pages, accessed January 11, 2011, http://
www.hubpages.com/hub/AMAZING_HUMAN_FACTS.
12. "Human Body Facts," Fun Shun, accessed January 17, 2011, http://www
.funshun.com/amazing-facts/human-body-facts.html.
13. "Amazing Facts about the Human Body," Buzzle, accessed January 17, 2011,
http://www.buzzle.com/articles/amazing-facts-about-the-human-body.html.
14. Ibid.

information as five volumes of *Encyclopaedia Britannica*. Your blood vessels laid end to end would be 60,000 miles long—enough to reach around the world twice. In just one square inch of skin, there are 4 yards of nerve fibers, 600 pain sensors, 1,300 nerve cells, 9,000 nerve endings, 36 heat sensors, 75 pressure sensors, 100 sweat glands, 3 million cells, and 3 yards of blood vessels.[15] If you have ever been pregnant, your uterus was able to expand up to 500 times its normal size to accommodate new life.[16] (By the way, stand amazed at your body and don't take the privilege of pregnancy lightly. It is the one time you are able to assist God in a miracle.) Not only do each of us have our own unique fingerprints, but no one else has a tongue print like you either![17] The list goes on and on. Your body is a marvel, and scientists are still trying to understand it all.

What a creation you are! Notice that in Psalm 139, David was worshipping the Lord because he was in awe of how his body was made. David didn't praise God because he was good looking or sported a chiseled physique, but he praised God for how He crafted him in fantastic and meticulous detail. He praised God that he was known personally and intimately by the Creator of the universe, and every day of his life had been thought about and prepared in love. Soak in this: God planned out

15. "Amazing Human Facts," Hub Pages, accessed January 11, 2011, http://www.hubpages.com/hub/AMAZING_HUMAN_FACTS.

16. "Human Body Facts," Fun Shun, accessed January 17, 2011, http://www.funshun.com/amazing-facts/human-body-facts.html.

17. "Amazing Human Facts," Hub Pages, accessed January 11, 2011, http://www.hubpages.com/hub/AMAZING_HUMAN_FACTS.

good works for you to do and be a part of even before you were born! Your body was made as His masterpiece, His work of art (Ephesians 2:10). I don't know about you, but no one has ever called me a work of art—maybe a piece of work, but never a masterpiece. Of all God's works, you are His most excellent.

David saw his body and wowed at its makeup, but notice also that when David looked at his body his focus shifted to the magnificence and majesty of God. "I thank you, High God—you're breathtaking!" Did you ever look at a waterfall, a sunset, or a baby's toothy grin, and marvel at God and the beauty of His handiwork? The design of your body warrants the same. Dawn, a very wise and insightful friend of mine, shared with me how one day Psalm 139 struck her in a fresh new way. She has always known that God knit her together and loves her wholeheartedly. But as she read these verses again, she realized God not only saw her strengths and good points when He was crafting her, but that He also saw her weaknesses, her imperfections, her struggles, and her flaws as well. And He still proceeded to create her. He did it with an unconditional, unfailing, lavish kind of love and joy because she was His. Her uniqueness, originality, and design were a reflection of God's mind, heart, and creativity. He created her and called her beautiful. Your body bears the name of the greatest Designer there is— the one and only God. Because of that fact alone, your body is absolutely beautiful and every moment calls out the majesty of God. This is the bigger picture.

Not only did God design our bodies but He made them for one specific purpose—for Himself. Colossians 1:16 (NIV) uses three important words to complete it: "all things were created through him *and for him*" (emphasis mine). And because all things are made through Him and for Him, they are sacred and have a value far beyond what our culture, and we personally, have deemed them to have. When we acknowledge we are His and give Him all of us, we can experience things far beyond what we ever imagined. Soak in these awesome truths about your body.

## Our bodies are members of Christ Himself.

All of us at one time or another, perhaps even now, have lived as though our bodies belong to us. Our focus has been on what we want, what we crave, what we think we need. Some of us may feel so lost or emotionally numb, we don't know what we need, so we succumb to anything in an attempt to find what we're looking for. That was me. At one point in my life I was desperately insecure with no direction, and looked for love in all the wrong places. I longed to be loved, desired, and to be that beautiful and treasured woman in someone's eyes. I became involved in the party scene and all that goes with it. The more I abused my body, the harder my heart became. I had little dignity, self-respect, or love for myself and no idea what my body was worth until one day, I realized my heart was numb and dying. Like a siren going off in my head, I realized the danger that nothing bothered me. It was then that God began to get my attention and start me on a journey of new life discovering who He was and what His heart held for me. I discovered that His love was the only thing that could fill my emptiness and my longing to be loved and treasured. Because of what Jesus did for me on the cross, I discovered that I had been beautiful in someone's eyes this whole time. They just happened to be God's. Discovering my identity through the eyes of Jesus not only changed my perspective but my life, and this was the pivotal point when I knew I was made for something greater.

I see young women today who are giving themselves away. I see scantily clad women on billboards and in magazines, and my heart breaks for them. Their bodies are beautiful, but I know their hearts are aching for something more to fill them. I hear about girls in high school and college who are sleeping with their boyfriends, and I long to whisper in their ear that they are meant for more. As a believer, your body is a member, a part of Jesus Christ Himself. That means that as a believer your body is "glued to" or "joined with" the Son of God at all times![18] Have you ever stopped to think how important your body is, or that it is an extension of Jesus Himself? You are His hands, His arms, His feet. Knowing this, how can we look at our bodies

18. Spiros Zodhiates, *The Complete Word Study Dictionary: New Testament* (Chattanooga, TN: AMG Publishers, 1992).

with the same eyes? Looking back, how I wish I would have known and believed this truth earlier in my life. I never experienced physical consequences from my poor choices, but emotionally and spiritually I felt the weight and limits of every single chain that I had bound myself in. For years, I swam in hurt, darkness, loneliness, and confusion. First Corinthians 6:15–18 (MSG) says, "Until that time, remember that your bodies are created with the same dignity as the Master's [Jesus'] body. You wouldn't take the Master's body off to a whorehouse, would you? . . . There's more to sex than mere skin on skin. Sex is as much spiritual mystery as physical fact. . . . Since we want to become spiritually one with the Master, we must not pursue the kind of sex that avoids commitment and intimacy, leaving us more lonely than ever. . . . In sexual sin we violate the sacredness of our own bodies, these bodies that were made for God-given and God-modeled love." Your body is beautiful because it is part of Jesus' body. Your body is meant for more.

> Our bodies are called home
> by God Himself, the Holy Spirit.

First Corinthians 6:19–20 (NIV) says, "Do you not know that your bodies are temples of the Holy Spirit, who is in you, whom you have received from God? You are not your own; you were bought at a price. Therefore honor God with your bodies." When you begin a new and living

relationship with Jesus, His Holy Spirit comes to live within you. Not just some of Him, but all of Him. Not only does He call your body a temple, but He calls your body the Holy of Holies, which houses God's presence—the holiest and most sacred place in the temple. In the Old Testament, absolutely no one was allowed in the Holy of Holies except the high priests, and they could only enter once a year. All the commoners like you and me worshipped God at a distance, in the temple courtyard. But because of Jesus, you don't have to stay at a distance anymore. His death paved the road for you and me to go right to the throne of God. His presence from heaven to your heart—that alone should make you stop in your tracks.

Inviting Jesus to make your heart His home changes the name on the deed. When Jesus died for you, He bought you with His life. That's how valuable you are. That's how full of love He is for you. Therefore, you don't own you anymore. You belong to Him. He has set you free from yourself! He owns you not to hinder you or stifle you, but to set you free to truly live! Because we are His home, we have the privilege of showing Him to the world. Our bodies are honored vessels to bring recognition to Him, to point to Him, to make Him known to those who are still bound up and enslaved to themselves. And you know the beauty of it? All we need to do is give Him access to every part of us and allow Him to reveal Himself. We don't have to do it in our own strength. We don't have to get it perfect, because we can't. When we give Him the reins, He will accomplish it through us! While Jesus was on earth, He glorified God, His Father. He spoke His words of truth, He lived out His heart, He loved unconditionally, He gifted His grace. Through Jesus we can see who God is, His character, His attributes, His message of forgiveness, redemption, and restoration. We get to do the same. We have the privilege of being a vessel of God Himself—allowing His Spirit to express Himself through us in showing His love, grace, and truth to everyone we know. Your body is meant for more.

> Our bodies are designed to worship Jesus, expressing love and gratitude toward Him.

Worship can take on many forms and the methods we think of right away are affiliated with music—singing, dancing, and playing musical instruments. I love music! And to hear my gifted friends, Lisa and Dawn, and the Circle of Friends Worship Team sing—they usher me into the throne room of heaven every time. Music is a beautiful form of worship, giving us an avenue to bring Jesus our thanks and praise.

Some of us associate worship as happening only in churches on Sunday mornings, and if we can't play an instrument or sing like an angel, we are out of luck. Fortunately, that's not true. We don't necessarily have to

be singing, strumming, or formally praying to worship Jesus. We don't have to be in a room full of people. You know why? Because genuine worship, the kind God wants, comes from the deepest part of us—our hearts, our affections, our spirits. We aren't pretending but are just being ourselves, giving Jesus who we are, wanting more of Him, and loving Him with all we have. Jesus told the Samaritan woman in John 4:23–24 (MSG), "It's who you are and the way you live that count before God. Your worship must engage your spirit in the pursuit of truth. That's the kind of people the Father is out looking for: those who are simply and honestly themselves before him in their worship. . . . Those who worship him must do it out of their very being, their spirits, their true selves, in adoration." To worship Jesus is to bow down to Him out of reverence, but what I love about this word *worship* is that it also refers to direction—moving forward, toward, or near something. The second part of this word *worship* means "to kiss."[19] God desires for us to move toward Him always, to be connected, stay close, to stay spiritually and emotionally intimate with Him. He wants our hearts, our love, our praise, our affections, our adoration—in essence, our worship. Anytime, anywhere—in the car or in the shower, on a hiking trail on Saturday or in a church on Sunday, sitting in a waiting room or lying in a hospital room. We can choose to worship on the mundane Mondays—while doing those everyday things that aren't flashy but that can be done with a heart of love and

19. Ibid.

worship for the One who has blessed us to overflowing. No matter where we are or what we are doing, we can bow our heads, our hearts, our very lives.

It was two o'clock in the morning and my friend's daughter startled her from sleep. Their pet chinchilla, Harley, had escaped from his cage and ended up snuggling into bed with her. To put Harley back in his cage was useless because he had chewed his way through the wire and would be eager to attempt his escape repeatedly throughout the night. Both knew their only option in order to get any sleep would be to retrieve another cage from the attic above the garage. In order to access the attic, both cars had to be moved out of the garage so they could use a ladder to climb into the attic. But being less than energetic at this time of the morning, my friend decided to skip the ladder option and to use her brute strength to simply hoist her daughter into the attic entry. Bending her knees and getting ready, she tucked her daughter's foot into her cupped hands and lifted her up with a mighty heave. Arms shaking and face contorted, my friend could only raise her a mere couple of inches. Her daughter, being the small and agile type that she is, was able to grab onto the sides of the entrance but proceeded to hang there in midair. As you can imagine, the laughter began, and from there it was all over. Regrouping, my friend assessed the situation. Where strength lacked, determination dominated. So, instructing her daughter to use her as a "springboard," my friend proceeded to climb onto the back of the truck's bed cover and get on her hands and knees. Her daughter, gathering as much speed as she could, literally jumped up and off Mom's back into the attic. Mission accomplished.

Obviously, not all of us will be in our garages at two o'clock in the morning using each other as trampolines. But, this story is a great word picture of what it means to worship God by serving one another using our bodies. Romans 12:1 (MSG) says, "So here's what I want you to do, God helping you: Take your everyday, ordinary life—your sleeping, eating, going-to-work, and walking-around life—and place it before God as an offering. Embracing what God does for you is the best thing you can do for him." We are to use our bodies to serve one another—in the inconvenient, even sacrificial moments of life. And in doing so, we are walking in the love and sacrifice Jesus demonstrated to us and for us. We are pointing to Him with our very lives. Our bodies were meant to worship, to declare the greatness of the only true and living God. Your body is meant for more.

> Our bodies are vehicles for carrying the love and encouragement of Jesus to all those we encounter.

We underestimate the power of encouragement and the role of being an encourager. To encourage others is to come alongside them, to help them by strengthening them. In ancient literature the word for encouragement was often used when speaking about military reinforcement in battle. How appropriate. Do you ever feel like you are in a battle firing away at the enemy—discouragement, despair, fear, anxiety, or the overwhelming and exhausting situations life can throw at you—and you're not sure how much longer you can hold on? Then beside you, one by one, fellow soldiers begin to emerge and hunker down for the fight. You are no longer alone and hope reappears.

The other day I was desperate to hear from the Lord. I was discouraged and flat-out frustrated. I went to bed with tears running down my face, asking Him for direction, and pouring out my heart to Him. I woke the next morning and read my Bible and confessed more of the sins of my heart to Him that His Word had shown me were there. Later that morning, I went to my computer and found a message awaiting me from a precious friend who had been praying for me that morning. She proceeded to tell me what the Lord had laid on her heart to share with me. It was incredible, and she didn't know anything that I had been wrestling with. God spoke directly to my heart through her. He had told me what I needed to hear, reminding me of who He is. God is the Master Encourager and uses willing and obedient vessels to share His messages—whether they are easy to hear or not, they are always motivated by love. I was so thankful she chose to intercede on my behalf and share that with me. It set me back on the path

He had called me to with a renewed clarity and focus. I realized that our encouragement to one another can be the difference between life and death, between hope and despair, between our choice to persevere or give up. Every day we have the opportunity to be a vessel of love and encouragement to someone by just "being there" and listening to someone who needs to talk. We can speak words based on God's truth that will build up, give life and strength, hope and promise. We can lend a smile, or reach out and touch the untouched. We can cheer one another on as we do life together. Practically showing Jesus to the world is giving with a pure heart and not expecting anything in return, or serving someone who needs help. It's offering a cup of water, either literally or figuratively, to those who are thirsty.

I will never forget the blazing-hot day in the ancient city of Petra in the Middle East. My friends and I were walking through the city when two little boys came running up to my friend and in broken English cried out, "Water! Water! Drink!" Looking over my shoulder, I saw my friend pouring water into this little boy's mouth, providing refreshment and the love of Jesus. All it took was five seconds. Using our bodies to show Jesus to the world is being a vehicle of God's love. It's doing another load of laundry, changing another diaper, going to the grocery store again. It's stopping to talk to the boss no one likes just to see how she's doing. And it's done all out of love. Not our love, because we don't possess a love like this. But out of the love that Jesus has given us and can fill us with.

My husband and I always remind couples we take

through premarital counseling that they have the beautiful privilege of demonstrating to a watching world the love of Jesus. How they love one another in their relationship can communicate the love that Jesus has for each one of us. So it is with you and me. We have an incredible opportunity to show a lost and searching world that the unconditional, unfailing, faithful love of Jesus is real. First John 3:16–18 (MSG) says, "This is how we've come to understand and experience love: Christ sacrificed his life for us. This is why we ought to live sacrificially for our fellow believers, and not just be out for ourselves. If you see some brother or sister in need and have the means to do something about it but turn a cold shoulder and do nothing, what happens to God's love? It disappears. And you made it disappear. My dear children, let's not just talk about love; let's practice real love." Your body is meant for more.

In Philippians 1, a missionary named Paul was in prison for telling others about Jesus. He was speaking of the possibilities of his near future—death or life—and the benefits of each. Verse 20 (NIV) stuck out to me like a neon light as I was thinking about our topic at hand. "I eagerly expect and hope that I will in no way be ashamed, but will have sufficient courage so that now as always CHRIST WILL BE EXALTED IN MY BODY, whether by life or by death" (emphasis mine). Every single reason you and your body exist—from your design to your purpose, from the moment He thought of you until you take your dying breath—is about Jesus. That is a high and sacred calling. That is a divine privilege. That is the bigger picture. You were meant for more.

# DISCUSSION QUESTIONS

1.  How have you tried to disguise or cover your imperfections? Were you satisfied with your results?

2.  Were you successful in "looking up" while reading this chapter? If not, what obstacles made it difficult? Did the obstacle relate to culture's way of thinking? How?

3.  Picture your favorite and most beautiful piece of creation. How does the truth impact you that you "take dibs" over ALL of creation—that you are God's most excellent work?

4.  Thinking about how you have lived, thought, or believed, who or what has your body belonged to up until now? Yourself, society, your peers, Hollywood, others?

5.  Which truths about your body brought you fresh insight? How so?

6.  Keeping in mind that our beliefs affect our thoughts, our thoughts affect our feelings, and our feelings impact our actions, what will you do with these truths? How will you choose to apply at least one of these truths?

7.  You were meant for more. How does this truth impact you?

# Notes

# Notes

# Notes

# Notes

# Notes

........................................................

........................................................

........................................................

........................................................

........................................................

........................................................

........................................................

........................................................

........................................................

........................................................

........................................................

........................................................

........................................................

........................................................

*Chapter 3*

## WHY DOES MY ARM KEEP WAVING AFTER MY HAND HAS STOPPED?

Charm is deceptive, and beauty
is fleeting; but a woman who
fears the Lord is to be praised.

PROVERBS 31:30 NIV

> Beauty is indeed a good gift of God; but that the good may not think it a great good, God disperses it even to the wicked.
>
> SAINT AUGUSTINE

Denise is one of those friends everyone should have the privilege of experiencing. She is absolutely hilarious. She called me on the phone the other day and challenged me to a dare. She dared me to take a handheld mirror, place it on the bathroom counter, and bend over the counter to look at my face in the mirror. She proceeded to tell me of her startling experience as she had done the same thing earlier that morning. So, I've got a dare for you. Take a handheld mirror, place it on your countertop, and bend over, looking into the mirror. What do you see? Where is your skin in relation to your face? Is it still hugging your bone structure nicely or hanging off in midair? Is gravity still your friend?

Some of us have always been dissatisfied with a certain body part since as long as we can remember.

Others of us who may have had some contentment, now have noticed a significant change in our bodies over time and are reeling in the wake of the "transformation." Whatever your position, you can know you are not alone. Listen to some quotes from friends of mine when asked about what funny surprises or body changes they have experienced:

"Since I breastfed my kids, I think they sucked everything out of me."

"My best friend and I fan through hot flashes at the same time. And the shock I experienced when I realized that gray hair appears other places than on my head!"

"The fact that my arm keeps waving good-bye after my hand has stopped, and even though I never played the trumpet, why is it that I can toot with the best of them?"

"My hair is getting thinner, my wrinkles are getting deeper, my lumps and bumps are getting lumpier and bumpier (and not all in the right places). AND as if that weren't bad enough. . .my son is going to college and will be a 'cougar.' I'm going to have to wear T-shirts that advertise that I am a cougar (yes, I'm in that age bracket)."

"My body temperature is headed north and my body parts are heading south! The hair on my head is thinning, while my upper lip is in need of hedge trimmers! How

does that happen? Why do men get better looking as they age and women just AGE?"

"I not only have 'rolls,' but full loaves of bread hanging off my hips and buttocks."

"When I WANT to be 'hot,' I'm usually cold."

"There are days that I can start out as Wonder Woman, and end up 'changing' quicker than the Incredible Hulk."

"When I laugh, sneeze, or cough, it usually means it's also time for a potty break."

"Cottage cheese should be on my plate, not my thighs."

"My short-term memory is shot. . .I can remember the PAST like it was yesterday. . .but TODAY, I can't remember yesterday."

One of my friends was reminded that she was developing flabby arms when she was playing with her dog and he jumped up and latched on to her "wings" with his teeth. Another one of my friends is trying to convince her mother-in-law that they should tattoo butterflies on the flabby part of their arms so when they wave, their butterflies actually fly.

Change happens. And if we haven't experienced it

yet, we will. Dr. Miller had some interesting things to say about why change happens. "Certainly, how each individual ages has a lot to do with how our cells are programmed from birth. As a matter of fact, genetics are likely the number one factor in how long you live and how young you look. But how we treat our bodies is also very important. Our bodies are exposed to toxins that accelerate aging, and they are exposed to healthy factors that hinder aging. Much of what we chalk up to 'getting older' is really us just becoming less active. Fatigue, poor sleep, weight gain, droopy body parts, decreased sex drive, arthritis, and many other conditions are indeed age related. But they are also very much related to exercise, eating well, and getting our rest. As we age, we tend to be less active and not work as hard physically. And sure enough, if you don't use it, you lose it. That rule applies to our body, our mind, our sex drive, and our spiritual life." Okay everybody, make sure you're "using it," because if we lost it who knows where we would even begin looking to find it.

I had the pleasure of talking to various women about changes they have experienced as they have gotten older, and most were initially saddened or frustrated. Change is unfamiliar; it's different. We don't know what to expect. It's a loss of what was. It's a loss of control we thought we had. One woman wondered why no one had warned her of these impending, inevitable changes. She became critical and scolded herself for not doing something sooner, yet despaired because she thought it was too late to begin.

Another woman stopped looking at herself in the mirror when getting out of the shower. If she was dressing and her husband came in, she would quickly try to cover herself so he wouldn't see her exposed. Desserts became a treat instead of routine as she recognized her body could no longer tolerate the extra calories or the way they made her feel physically. Some began to exercise. One woman began working out at age forty-eight and loved the results she saw. One lady who didn't want to transition from contacts to glasses finally realized she needed to choose practicality over her perception of beauty. So she picked one of the trendiest pairs she liked and put her pride on the shelf. Another woman dealt with her realization of change by turning her focus to an area of fulfillment and purpose in her life that she enjoyed. Not a single lady was enthused when change began, but while some chose not to let it dominate, others were more negatively impacted. Some never liked their bodies because of past abuse, some because of chronic health conditions. Like the others, they initially grieved, but their negative body image continued to affect their attitude as a whole, which in turn affected all areas of their life. Culture hasn't helped. It says that we must do everything possible to save ourselves from this downward spiral of physical destruction and demise. And once change occurs, it's all downhill from there.

There is no question, we all need to deal with change—and sooner than we thought. Dr. Miller gave me some eye-opening news that our body tissues are already starting to decline in our late twenties or early thirties, and after menopause there is a rapid shift. He says as we age our muscle is naturally replaced by fat, which slows down our metabolism, burning fewer calories. However, when change comes there are some excellent ways we can care for ourselves and perhaps attain visible results. We can choose to exercise regularly, get adequate rest, or eat smaller portions and make healthier choices. Dr. Miller, a strong advocate of exercise, says exercise builds and maintains our muscles keeping our metabolism higher even while we are sitting on the couch watching TV. However, he also admits that even with exercise, our body changes on a cellular level with age, and it's not for the better. There are things that will change that we simply cannot control. This makes the battle against change not impossible, but definitely harder. There are the God-given parts that we have been discouraged by for years—large noses, wide hips, curly hair, poker-straight hair, small breasts, big breasts, thin lips, dimpled thighs, you name it. There are also the trouble spots that come with age—diminished eyesight, weight gain, droopiness and dryness, wrinkles and white hair, age spots, muffin tops, and varicose veins—and even other changes we never planned on.

At age thirty-five, a friend of mine found a lump in her breast, which resulted in a mastectomy that same year. She was a single parent facing her grief and loss very much alone. At first, all she could think about was her

desire to be healthy again, to be cancer-free, to be there for her daughter. But as she came through those initial concerns, she became more and more aware that she was a woman with only one breast. At times she joked with others in her insecurity that she was only "part woman," but on a deeper level, she wondered that if she ever met a man that she wanted to marry, how would he react when she told him the truth about her body? There were days she felt angry that she had experienced breast cancer, that she was now deemed "deformed." She wondered what others thought, if they could tell she had only one real breast.

Several years later, she met a man and as their relationship grew, they began to talk about marriage. So, for her peace of mind, she wanted to tell him about her previous bout with cancer and her resulting surgery. His response to her news was not only a relief, but one of freedom and hope. "Why would that matter? It's what is on the inside that I care about." The two married and six years later, her routine mammogram revealed another tumor, which turned out to be cancer once again. Facing cancer for the second time wasn't easy, but she says losing her other breast wasn't as difficult. She knew her husband loved her for who she was. Several years later, doctors found a suspicious-looking tumor on her ovary, calling for another surgery to remove her uterus and ovaries.

Experiencing cancer multiple times was difficult, but through the journey she has grown and matured, learning that physical beauty is a fleeting thing. She testifies that

she now has peace because she has chosen it. She may not have control over the changes that have occurred without, but she has changed her focus and knows she can change what is within. As a lover of God and a woman who has lived this life lesson, she comments, "A lot of women think they will be noticed with tight clothes or plummeting necklines, when in reality the real attraction is the look on their face, their smile, their attitude, the way they convey themselves to others. To me, it's a lie to think the real attraction is all physical, because I have experienced something else."

Several years ago, I had the privilege of working as a chaplain at a continuing-care retirement community. I remember quickly discovering that life isn't fair and that change is no respecter of persons. I watched a wife who was wasting away in every sense of the word, and her husband who came to visit every day. This isn't what retirement was supposed to be like. I watched a once-vibrant registered nurse who now lay in her bed for the eleventh year, unable to talk, walk, or do anything for herself. I listened to a woman affected by Alzheimer's who recounted the joys of her earlier years, describing a husband who loved her wholeheartedly, but only to yell out in frustration when she couldn't remember his name. I listened to a man with Parkinson's describe his struggle as he lost his ability to do things, to think and speak, as he lost the value that he had always assigned himself. I can "do," therefore I am someone of value. That's culture's

thinking. And it's ours, too. My question is, what if we can't do? Have we lost our value? What if I can't walk anymore, am I useless? What if I don't have the taut body of a twenty-year-old anymore, am I ugly? What if I have crow's-feet around my eyes, is that what everyone sees? So, several questions beg to be asked. How do we deal with change? How do we deal with things out of our control? How do we make peace with the things we don't like?

We may not always have a choice as to the change that comes, but we do have a choice as to how we will deal with it. Just like with anything else in life, we can choose to react or respond when it comes. This is an area where God has me focused and practicing right now. It is something I obviously have needed for a while, however.

My kids and I were in a rush and running late to church, falling all over each other trying to climb into the family van. As the boys were smacking each other in the backseat, I was slamming the gearshift into REVERSE and yelling at the top of my lungs, "QUIT HITTING EACH OTHER AND LEARN YOUR BIBLE VERSES!" That probably wasn't the best way to go about it. Obviously, my heart needed a Bible verse or two. Even as I was yelling at them to learn their verses, I recognized the idiocy of my reactive behavior and the irony of the situation and laughed at myself. However, if I'm honest, in most situations my first inclination is to react. Reacting is based in emotion—whatever that transient and intense feeling may be at the moment. It is being emotionally

out of control. If someone says something that I don't like or that is hurtful, my first reaction is to become defensive. I may retort with a curt or angry reply, attempt to explain myself, or withdraw altogether. Reacting is not the most mature response, if you haven't gathered that yet. Responding, however, is based in truth. It is stopping yourself, keeping the bigger perspective, and choosing to be emotionally controlled with a goal to assess the situation with insight and wisdom.

Proverbs 31:30 says that beauty is fleeting—here and gone, just like that. Confirmation lies in 1 Peter 3:3–6, which says that a woman's beauty shouldn't depend on her outward appearance, that for a woman who loves the Lord—her beauty comes from within. Our outward beauty fades, but this genuine beauty doesn't. This beauty comes from a quiet, still, and gentle spirit—a spirit that doesn't react out of our emotion but responds out of His peace. *To be still* means we possess a spirit that is undisturbed and, better yet, is described as "keeping one's seat."[20] How many times have I jumped out of my seat, either physically or emotionally, in reaction or alarm? How many times has my husband advised me to just "sit on" something before making a decision? Responding is "staying in our seat," not necessarily staying quiet but discerning and asking God when and how to speak, when and what to do. It is a heart that is humble, does what is right, and does not give way to fear. Fear of disaster, fear of death, or even a fear of growing older doesn't

---

20. Ibid.

move this woman to react because she trusts in her God who is far bigger. Beauty lies in a woman who fears the Lord, a woman who loves and reverences Jesus Christ, who submits to Him as Lord of her life and lover of her soul. Nothing can extinguish the beauty of Jesus Christ radiating from within, no matter how many changes our body may experience. When everything else falls away, He is what remains.

The bigger picture is that Jesus is our beauty. As physical change may be affecting us outwardly, He is beautifying us inwardly in character and faith. He gives us a confidence that doesn't even compare to what we can glean from our accomplishments or achievements. It is a confidence based on who He is and the work He is doing within us to make us who He has called us to be. Have you ever seen a woman who may not be physically attractive by the world's standards, but she is absolutely beautiful because of her joy, the way she carries herself, and loves people? Have you ever seen anyone glow? That beauty emanates from within and is "Jesus beauty." In the same way, have you ever seen a physically attractive woman, and you get to know her and find she isn't so attractive anymore? Proverbs 11:22 (NIV) says, "Like a gold ring in a pig's snout is a beautiful woman who shows no discretion." Without Jesus and His attributes in us, beauty isn't genuine beauty.

*Reacting* to change is reacting out of emotion, being extreme, setting goals we can never reach, or devising a plan that we could never stick to. *Reacting* to change is

submitting to a defeated attitude, continually meditating on the negative, or writing ourselves out of life and activities because we are "too ugly" or "too old." *Reacting* to change is trying to assert control where we don't have it, affecting ourselves and especially others around us. So, what are some things we can think about as we calmly "remain seated" emotionally when change comes? For those who have been gifted with a natural bent toward a positive personality, this may come a little easier, but it always comes down to a choice no matter how we're wired.

1. Reacting is trying to assert control where we don't have it, but responding is recognizing where we do have control, taking responsibility, and doing what we can.

2. Responding is acknowledging it would be nice if our body parts weren't changing but realizing what we have. What blessings surround us? What are we focusing on?

3. Responding is opening our eyes to a new perspective. We may not appreciate the different look of some parts, but is there a way we can treat them with care? Not for them obviously, because they don't have a clue, but for us. For our mind-set, for our attitude. Usually if we don't like something, we tend to ignore or hide it because we don't want to draw attention

to it. We don't go out of our way or honor it in any way. What if we did? For example, we may have saggy parts. What about going out and buying very pretty lingerie to wear? For our dimpled thighs or flabby arms, why not schedule a massage regularly or begin toning them with a weight workout? For our seemingly ugly toes or breaking nails, we could schedule a pedicure or manicure every so often. It's something we can do to love, honor, and take care of the changing parts. We just may learn to appreciate them.

4. Responding may be looking at our body as a vehicle taking us through life. My dear friend Jeni told me she sees the changes she has experienced as badges of honor and courage awarded her due to giving birth to her children. She looks at them as representing all the years of choices made, decisions handled, tears shed, people moving in and out of her life, every hardship, every celebration, every single life experience she's had that has brought her to where she is today. While some would say their bodies are broken down and tired, she would say hers is just "lived in" and experienced. And she respects her body because of it.

5. Responding is asking ourselves what body parts the Bible mentions often and focuses on. Our hands, feet, eyes, mind, mouth, and heart to name a few.

Why then do we focus on all the body parts our culture does? Song of Songs (4:1–7) does mention a woman's breasts, lips, teeth, hair, and neck, and they are painted beautifully. It would be safe to deduce that this man's loving adoration comes not because of this woman's physical perfection, but because of the way he sees her and the intimacy they share. This woman had darkened skin from the sun, which wasn't considered desirable, because she was made to take care of the family vineyards. She admits because of the work, she has neglected taking care of her body (vv. 5–6).[21] I truly wonder what size tunic she wore and am pretty sure by the way he's swooning that he didn't even care. But I'm willing to bet based on other cultures' perceptions of beauty today, that she was nowhere close to a size 4.

6.  Responding is looking at Jesus. I always thought it interesting that scripture describes Jesus as average looking. Isaiah 53:2 (NIV) says, "He had no beauty or majesty to attract us to him, nothing in his appearance that we should desire him." Then why do we find Jesus always surrounded by large crowds of people? Since a boy, scripture says He grew in favor with God and men (Luke 2:52). Jesus taught with authority, boldness, and conviction; He loved like no other, healed miraculously, and lived the desires of His Father's heart. People were drawn to Him.

21 Ibid.

Yes, He was God in flesh and we are not. But as believers, His Spirit lives just as powerfully within each of us. If the Son of God was not handsome physically but attracted multitudes for His kingdom's purposes by who He was, why and how does our focus become skewed so easily? Who are we living for? What is our purpose in impacting others?

When I asked women what helped them through the transition of bodily change, every single one who responded in a healthy way said it was their faith. One woman said she likes her body now more than she ever has in her life, not necessarily because of the way it looks but because she has fallen in love with Jesus, and she holds within her His peace and acceptance. Another woman shared that because of her relationship with Jesus she could accept that her body was transitioning and not turning heads anymore. She could appreciate the beauty of youth but acknowledged that there was still a beauty to be had. She was ready to embrace the beauty of growing older with grace. Women shared that having supportive and loving husbands helped tremendously, but it was their relationship with Jesus that made all the difference.

My older friend was sitting in her chair; the lady I once knew was now gone. Years earlier, I had visited her but in her home when she knew who I was. She realized her dementia was progressing, but she told me that there was one thing she would never forget—that Jesus had always

been with her. Now, every time I visited with her, I shared that favorite memory and she would smile. On this day, I read familiar scriptures to her and sang, and she joined right in. They were words I couldn't understand, but God heard every one distinctly. As I began to pray, tears rolled down my cheeks as I was touched by God's Spirit and the realization that she felt Him, too. Her eyes were closed and she was joining me in prayer. Paul's words from Romans 8 (NIV) came to my mind and I prayed, "For I am convinced that neither death nor life, neither angels nor demons. . .neither height nor depth. . ." And as I prayed, I included, "*neither sickness nor health* can 'separate us from the love of God.' " In those moments, the power and intimacy, the worship and communion with the Lord and with each other was absolutely precious. He was far bigger than any change that had come her way. As I reached over to give her a hug, she kissed my cheek. This day there was no church building, no sermon, but a party of only two who had just experienced God in true worship. Her body may have changed, but her Jesus had not. He shone through her, and she was absolutely beautiful. Change may find us, but it doesn't define us.

# DISCUSSION QUESTIONS

1. What areas regarding body image have been your most challenging—those you were born with, changes that that have come with age, or changes you never planned on?

2. What are some of the changes you have noticed in your body (include most surprising if you would like)?

3. What was your response to these changes? How have these changes affected your thoughts? Attitude? General outlook on life?

4. Do you tend to react or respond to life? Discuss various examples from your own life of reacting versus responding. What have you discovered?

5. Discuss the various points mentioned in regard to responding. Which thought resonates with you the most?

6. What things have helped you get through the transition of change?

7. How will you practically apply and practice responding to change?

8.  Do you recognize that if you have a relationship with Jesus that you have a beauty that cannot be extinguished? You, my sister, are beautiful. How will you choose to respond to this truth?

# Notes

# Notes

# Notes

# Notes

........................................................................

........................................................................

........................................................................

........................................................................

........................................................................

........................................................................

........................................................................

........................................................................

........................................................................

........................................................................

........................................................................

........................................................................

........................................................................

# Notes

*Chapter 4*

## YOU MEAN I GET A SERVANT WITH THIS HOUSE?

Do you not know that in a race all the runners run, but only one gets the prize? Run in such a way as to get the prize. Everyone who competes in the games goes into strict training. They do it to get a crown that will not last, but we do it to get a crown that will last forever.

1 CORINTHIANS 9:24–25 NIV

> I have to exercise early in the
> morning before my brain
> figures out what I'm doing.

ANONYMOUS

At her annual physical, my friend waited in the room anticipating the pleasure of visiting with her gynecologist. As she waited, the nurse practitioner entered the room with my friend's chart in hand. As she reviewed the information listed there, she proceeded to tell her patient that "at her age" she now needed to eat smaller portions but eat more frequently throughout the day. The nurse also looked at her and declared she also needed to be doing cardiovascular exercise five times a week. As the nurse practitioner continued for the next couple of minutes, she repeated "CARDIOVASCULAR EXERCISE FIVE TIMES A WEEK" at least four times. My friend, who is a very busy mother with little ones still at home, was thinking in her mind that exercising five times a week was like telling her to move to China and learn Chinese.

She can't even go to the bathroom by herself, let alone have the energy, desire, or time to exercise. She looked at her nurse and finally said rather emphatically, "I hear you," just so her resounding declaration would cease. As my friend recounted her story to me, she said she realized later that as the nurse had been encouraging her in physical fitness, her gown had been open. She said, "There I was, thinking my gown was tied when all was exposed—my flabby belly and sagging breasts down to my knees. No wonder she pushed the exercise."

*Exercise.* Many of us hear the word and either shudder or roll our eyes. I know I have. Have you ever stopped to wonder why that is? What is it about exercise that we don't like? For me, the most prominent reason I have failed to exercise is, it hurts. Second, it takes motivation. Those two reasons alone could make up my entire list, and they would be enough. But I'll continue. Number three, when we hear others talking about how they are caring for themselves, and we aren't necessarily, it produces feelings of guilt or even shame. Can anybody relate to this one? Obviously, those aren't pleasant feelings so we tend to stay away or remove ourselves from the issue that caused them. For some of us, when we hear people that are seemingly obsessed with health, we justify our lack of care by saying that we don't even want to start exercising if we are going to become like that. But I've never thought that, of course. Number four, it can get discouraging. If we don't see the results we desire, we chalk it up as useless and stop. Number five, there is no way I can fit one more thing into my day. And number six, we just don't want to. It isn't fun. It's monotonous and boring. We want to do what we want to do and when we want to do it. We don't want people telling us what we need or have to do. I'm sure you can make your own list as to why you may chalk up exercise right up there with torture. No matter our reasons, we can't argue with the fact that exercise is good for us. We will hit on exercise, but the focus of this chapter is about servanthood. However, not in the way you may imagine.

Because our bodies are a valuable gift, to care for them is an act of love and respect—to God, to others, and to ourselves. Self-care can look like a variety of things— exercise, balanced nutrition, massage therapy, a time-out for mom locked away in a quiet room, eight hours of great sleep, or doing something you thoroughly enjoy. Did I mention massage therapy? We know we should do it and it's good for us, but self-care can be a difficult thing to do. As I've thought about this, I've wondered what it would be like if my friend graciously let me borrow her car for the day and I trashed it with food and wrappers, spilled coffee all over the seats, then ran into the guard-rail a couple of times. When I took it back, I would thank her for its use, hand over the keys, and leave without saying a word. I may wonder how that would go, but I would never actually do it. I am horrified if I have a fender bender in my own car. So why wouldn't I take care of something far more precious given to me by someone far more important who loves me far greater? It's something I think about.

Our bodies need care but the Bible says they also need care but the Bible says they also
need control and discipline. Ouch. And I know that many of you who just read the word *discipline* are tempted to close this book. But stick with me. I'm talking about training our body out of a love for God. Scripture says self-control is for our protection (Proverbs 25:28; 1 Peter 5:8). It's a training that enables us to say "no" to ourselves when needed and say "yes" to what is best for us—a body that is willing, surrendered, and available for God's use. Disciplining our bodies can cover a gamut of areas. If we tend to be workaholics, consistently fall into the captivity of activity, or get overwhelmed by the busyness of life, discipline may mean intervals of much-needed rest. If we struggle with indulging ourselves in spending or eating, it may mean scaling back and saying no to our wants— be it a designer purse or more mashed potatoes. If we are known to say the first thing that comes to our mind, it may mean thinking before we speak, speaking with gentleness, or shutting our mouths altogether. Discipline may mean watching what images we put into our minds, or focusing first on the positive in a situation, as opposed to the negative. Do you remember in chapter one when I said we need to ask ourselves some tough questions about our bodies and perspectives? And that it's okay, even vital, that we are transparent with ourselves and with God? So, here's a question for you to answer honestly. What or who is controlling your body? For some of us it may be food, either eating too much or too little. It may be excessive exercise or the comfy living-room couch. Is it nonstop

activity? Some of us may struggle with cutting our bodies or giving them away. If we aren't married, we may have given ownership of our bodies to someone else who has no rights to it. Some of us may be controlled by various drugs, alcohol, or by the perfection standard we've talked about—having to look or perform a certain way to feel accepted, beautiful, or significant. And all of us have bodies controlled by our minds. So what's consuming your mind? Is it guilt, negativity, anxiety, fantasy, fear, anger? Our bodies are controlled by something, whether it is one of these things or the Holy Spirit. We just need to be real and name it so we know where we are and what we're dealing with.

One tool to train our bodies is through exercise. It is a great way to care for our bodies physically, but it does wonders for us mentally as well. Exercise provides an outlet for built-up stress and also develops mental tenacity. My friend of thirty-three years, whom I love dearly, is a disciplined woman. And she has to be, because Julie runs half marathons. Julie told me what she needs to do to prepare for her races—care for her body through appropriate nutrition, run so many miles regularly, get adequate rest, and wear proper shoes. But to run a marathon she not only relies on her physical preparedness but her mental toughness as well. She told me, "If you don't have the proper mind-set, you won't complete the race. The race involves both mental and physical toughness. I can dress like a runner and never run a day in my life. On the outside you would think I run, but if you would see me try and run a mile I would collapse. You need endurance to run the race. Reaching your goal will depend on how and how hard you train." Julie has always been a natural athlete ever since we were young. She was one of the fastest runners, one of the hardest throwers, best hitters, and greatest shooters. Julie succeeded often because of her God-given talent, but ultimately, she succeeded because of her tenacity. She worked hard and did not give up. Endurance is what gets us across the finish line.

Now, my exercise pattern in the past has been to work out for several months then stop for several years. Yes, I said years. After several *years*, the motivation returns once again, and I go full tilt until my schedule crowds it out or I get tired and unmotivated. Obviously, discipline in this regard was never one of my strong points. However, I have started to exercise again, but this time with a different perspective. As I began, it wasn't fun as I huffed and puffed through my workout and woke with sore muscles for the first little while. Whenever I was in the midst of push-ups, I understood what Paul was saying in 1 Corinthians 9 when he talked about training to the point of agony. Yeah, for me that was push-ups. But this time around I have come to value what exercise does. Exercise is developing mental tenacity in me, mental stick-to-itiveness so that I can go the distance. When I get out of breath, tenacity tells me to keep going. When my abs are burning, tenacity tells me there's only five more. When I feel like I'm going to drop over, tenacity tells me I can drop over in another minute, but for now, I'm mastering my body. The focus has turned from losing weight to the bigger picture of better health. The focus has turned from being approved of by others to the bigger picture of being responsible for taking care of God's dwelling place. The focus has changed from seeing my body as master to the bigger picture of seeing my body as a servant. Have you ever thought of your body that way? For so long, we have allowed our body to control us and be our master, giving it whatever it wants even to our detriment. But your body was gifted to you as a servant for you to use to bless the Lord and others, for you to love and appreciate, for you to accomplish the great purposes the Lord has called you to. Isn't that cool?

In 1 Corinthians 9:24–27, Paul talks about a runner, one that in our day would be comparable to an Olympian or marathon runner. He runs his race with diligence, not just running the race to say he competed, but running the race to win. He trains for the race and practices hard. He works his body into shape, running until it hurts. He wrestles, fights, and makes every effort to achieve his goal despite all the obstacles along the way. And as he trains for the race he practices self-control, so he doesn't do anything to ruin his chances of winning that first-place prize. Paul speaks of a runner, but he is likening him to you and me. He compares the race he's talking about to the race we're running, this race called life. The race of life isn't easy and can even be grueling. Around each bend there can be another distraction detouring us from staying the course, let alone running to win. Because life is more than just getting through a workout, it's getting through trials, times of waiting, disappointments, frustrations, and heartbreak. But these times aren't spent in vain when we bring them before Jesus. He can turn tragedy into tenderness, pain into patience, failure into faith, struggle into surrender, trial into tenacity, temptation into triumph. So, how do we train physically and spiritually? Be intentional, stay focused, and make our bodies servants.

## Being Intentional

Several years ago I had the privilege of walking with two close friends in a breast cancer fundraising walk in memory of my friend's mother. The goal was to walk sixty miles in three days, so we were provided a guideline of how to train months before the event. Two of us, who are a little more goal oriented, began training right away. We were intentional about scheduling training into our routine because we wanted our feet to be in the best shape possible. We had heard all kinds of horror stories about blisters developing and toenails falling off after the walk. If you started with blisters after the first day of walking, the next two would be miserable, and finishing the walk questionable. The other third of our little group is more of a free spirit, and the comic relief in our group, reminding us that life doesn't always have to be so serious. Needless to say, we all balance each other out, which is a lot of fun.

But because of her more laissez-faire approach to life, she trained when she had time, but otherwise she really wasn't too worried about it.

The weekend arrived and the first twenty miles went pretty well for my friend. However, at the end of the second day, I was popping a blister under one of her toenails while she nursed more on her heel. By the end of the third day, she was sitting in the medical tent getting her feet bandaged so she could finish the walk. We, as her closest friends, stood beside her, showing nothing but support as we waited patiently and laughed at her. But she knew our hearts, received it well, and laughed right along with us. It turns out she lost several toenails later at home but didn't realize it until her kids found them lying on the living-room floor. The training for the race wasn't fun or convenient, but the lessons we learned and the time we had together were worth every cramp, sore muscle, and blister we experienced. With intentionality in training, we got the job done. We set a goal and marked out a plan in order to attain the goal.

Being intentional with physical exercise or self-control is making the decision ahead of time. It is no longer "just talking about it," but doing something about it. Maybe that means deciding ahead of time you won't go back for seconds or spend over a certain amount. When you feel overwhelmed, you will call a friend to talk and process your feelings rather than withdrawing and "stuffing" them. If you want to get in shape physically, you decide in advance and write "exercise" on your calendar, just like you would a social event. Start with three days a week or something that you can stick to and maintain. And get creative with what you do. You can work out alone or with someone else, making it easier to stick to and more fun.

The spiritual race we are running requires the same intentionality. Intentionally take some time every day and spend it reading God's Word and praying throughout the day. Or perhaps take two hours out of your week to invest in someone else. Maybe that means choosing to love someone ahead of time, knowing he or she may say something annoying or hurtful. It may mean choosing to respond based on godly character rather than react out of our human emotion when something doesn't go our way. Paul says in 1 Corinthians 9:26 that he doesn't run aimlessly but with intentionality. He has made up his mind and knows where he's going. He keeps his head up and his eyes fixed on the finish line, not even glancing at the distractions along the way that will pull him off course. Jesus has called us to live with purpose for a purpose—Him and the work He gave us to do.

## Staying Focused

Once we've set the goal and have set up the plan, then we strive to stay focused in carrying it out. Where our eyes are fixed is vital, because everything else in us will follow suit. I have a friend who has struggled with her perception of food. In the past, she has turned to food as something to satisfy her desire for entertainment, boredom, frustration, or any other all-consuming feeling she experienced. She allowed those feelings at the moment to dictate bingeing episodes. In turning over this issue to the Lord, He showed her she was being deceived and that she needed to see the food not as she perceived it to be, but for the reality of what it really is: fats, protein, sugars, fiber, and various nutrients. He showed her food was made for her nourishment and to be enjoyed, but to be consumed by it was sinful. What God had given her to enjoy, she had turned into a weapon in the hands of Satan and her own desire. She authentically shares that keeping proper focus isn't always easy, but the Lord is helping her to do just that. When she changes her focus to what is true, the power of the craving for food is broken. She says, "I don't need to be deceived into a lustful relationship with food because I see clearly what reality is and how it will affect my body."

It is no different for any of us. Every single one of us has dealt with all-consuming feelings and been deceived. We may fall for the lie by turning to another man for fulfillment because of an emotional connection. But when we see things as they really are and contemplate playing with fire, we will see inevitable destruction and pain to ourselves and others. We may live in discontentment, spending our days longing for what could be and missing out on what is. When we see things for what they really are we stand amazed at the thousands of blessings that lie right in front of us. We may be tempted to cut our bodies again to cope with our emotional pain, but when we see things for what they really are we are reminded that Jesus bled once so we don't have to anymore. It may be lies about insecurity, perfection, or that we are all alone and no one understands. It can be anything that blinds us to truth. When our eyes aren't on Him, they will be on us, and we lose focus very quickly, taking us dangerously off course. To master our bodies, we pray for the Holy Spirit's perspective to see things as they really are. As He shows us that truth through His Word, we can believe it! We then choose to keep our hearts and eyes fixed on truth. This is where our mental toughness kicks in, blocking out how we feel or what others are saying if not aligned with God's truth. This is where "how we train determines how we finish." Proper focus builds endurance.

Seeing things as they really are includes looking at the way we are caring for or controlling ourselves and deciphering if we feel conviction or shame. Many of us feel shame and guilt, and we want to hide. We will hear condemning kinds of statements in our minds about the way we look, that there is no way we will ever gain control over our bodies or those things we struggle with. Shame and condemnation are not from the Holy Spirit (Romans 8:1), so we need to guard against pulling away from Him, becoming hopeless and distracted and lured off course. Conviction, on the other hand, is from the Holy Spirit, and its purpose is always to drive us toward Jesus, setting us back on course. Hope always accompanies conviction. Perhaps we haven't been caring for our bodies well and we feel the strong urge that it's time to make some changes to master our bodies. Jesus can help us do that. Jesus loves you like no one else can or ever has. He wants you, no matter how dissatisfied you are with yourself. When we give Him all of us, we can trust Him to lead us to a new place of health and life—physically, mentally, emotionally, and spiritually—in His time and in His way.

In 1 Corinthians 9:25–26, Paul says he was running to win the crown that will last forever, the reward of eternity with Jesus and doing what God had called him to do. He had a goal that he stayed focused on. He didn't punch the air in wild abandon, but his punches were strategic, timely, and on target. His focus paid off. He persevered, and God brought him safely and victoriously to the finish line. Paul, with the power of the Holy Spirit, mastered his body to do the work for which Jesus had made him. It can be the same for us. Training ourselves is seeing things for what they are and focusing on truth.

## Making Our Bodies Servants

Training means we choose to look and treat our bodies as servants, no longer as masters. This means exercising self-restraint and not giving in to our every want or craving. At first it is difficult but then gets easier as we train, and finally our body is brought under control. In putting our bodies through the "stress" of training, we will experience change. As we get older, it may not be losing ten pounds, but it may mean a healthier heart, more energy, and feeling better. As we experience life, it may not be the situation we would have chosen, but it may mean a closer, more intimate walk with Jesus that we wouldn't trade. Paul said in 1 Corinthians 9:27 (NIV), "I strike a blow to my body and make it my slave so that after I have preached to others, I myself will not be disqualified for the prize." Paul is making his body his servant so he can "walk the talk"! Paul doesn't just want to tell others what they need to do, he was determined to do the same! His desire was to live out his faith out of his love for Jesus. As a Pharisee, before Paul followed Jesus, he thought he was doing the right thing. His heart was hardened and empty and his motivations steeped in following the rules. He completely missed the mark. In developing self-control, what if our motivations weren't based in hollow discipline but in a love relationship with Jesus? When we love God we will obey Him (John 14:21), not because we have to, but because we want to. The truth is our bodies can be trained in every way. Many of us have believed that it just isn't possible. We have failed all too often with diets, exercise, and other forms of self-control. We have given in to our addictions repeatedly. As a believer, self-control is something that the Holy Spirit produces in us (Galatians 5:22–23), and it can grow in ever-increasing measure (2 Peter 1:8). He does the transforming work, but we need to choose at every moment to let Him do it. Second Peter 1:3 (NIV) promises, "His divine power has given us everything we need for a godly life through our knowledge of him who called us by his own glory and goodness." We don't have to do this alone anymore. It is God's power that sets us free through Jesus. He has made available everything we need to live the life He has planned for us—not just any ordinary life but abundant and overflowing life!

Keep in mind, we all struggle with various things, but whatever it is, we need to acknowledge there is a battle going on. Paul said in Romans 7 that he does things he doesn't want to do. He wants to do good things, but he doesn't always succeed at accomplishing it. Boy, can I relate. Paul says he's got a sinful nature and nothing good lives in him apart from Jesus Christ. The same goes for you and me. We will always battle our sinful nature. However, because of Jesus who died for us and rose again, conquered sin and guilt, and declared us as innocent, sin no longer masters us. We can choose to sin, but sin doesn't have to control us any longer. We have been set free by His grace. The sinful nature, the temptations, the struggles will always be there, but we can control how we respond to them. We can choose to use our bodies for the glory of God. Ladies, you were meant to win the race. And guess who stands at the finish line? Jesus Himself, eyes bright with joy, a beautiful smile, and open arms waiting for you to jump into them. He's been praying for you, drawing you to Himself, and cheering you on the entire time. His heart has always been for you.

# DISCUSSION QUESTIONS

1. Are you running the race of life to say you competed or are you running to win? What makes you answer the way you did?

2. How have you looked at exercise or self-control in the past? What have been your reasons or motivations for training?

3. If your motivation for self-control was love for Jesus, how would that change your mind-set, choices, and actions?

4. Who or what is controlling your body?

5. How do you feel God calling you to specifically train?

6. How does the truth impact you that your body is your servant rather than your master? How does it change your perspective? How can you apply this truth in your personal training?

7. "Exercise daily in God—no spiritual flabbiness, please! Workouts in the gymnasium are useful, but a disciplined life in God is far more so, making you fit both today and forever" (1 Timothy 4:7–8 MSG). In what practical ways can you become intentional

and formulate a plan in your personal training both physically and spiritually?

8. "To master our bodies, we pray for the Holy Spirit's perspective to see things as they really are." How does this statement apply to your life? Where have your eyes been focused? Spend time praying that you will receive the Holy Spirit's eyes to see what is real and what God wants to show you.

# Notes

........................................................

........................................................

........................................................

........................................................

........................................................

........................................................

........................................................

........................................................

........................................................

........................................................

........................................................

........................................................

........................................................

........................................................

........................................................

# Notes

# Notes

# Notes

# Notes

# Notes

## Chapter 5

### WHEN THE TENT BEGINS TO SAG, KEEP YOUR EYES ON THE MANSION

We've been given a glimpse of the real thing, our true home, our resurrection bodies! The Spirit of God whets our appetite by giving us a taste of what's ahead. He puts a little of heaven in our hearts so that we'll never settle for less.

2 Corinthians 5:5 msg

> People are like stained-glass windows.
> They sparkle and shine when the sun is
> out, but when the darkness sets in,
> their true beauty is revealed only
> if there is a light from within.
>
> ELISABETH KÜBLER-ROSS

All those who like to camp, please raise your hands. I think camping is a wonderful premise for spending time in the great outdoors with family and friends, getting away from the hurriedness of the regular routine, the opportunity to return to "simpler living" by cooking over an open fire, setting up tents, and just being together. I think that sounds wonderful, but unfortunately for me, doing it isn't so wonderful. Years ago, before our sons were born, my husband and I were invited to go on a camping trip with another couple. Thankfully, they were expert campers because this was going to be our first experience. We were really looking forward to going and getting away for some relaxation and fun. We arrived

at our campsite, which was situated on the sands of a riverbank. We set up our tents, hung our clothesline, and made ourselves at home. We were going to be there an entire week, and we were thrilled.

As the week played itself out, overall we were enjoying ourselves. Neither my husband nor I are much for insects, sweltering heat and humidity, sand in our bed, or nearby gators in the river, but we tried to make fun of ourselves and laugh our way through. That is, until the storm hit. I woke to the sound of booming thunder and water dripping on my face. Our tent had become a sieve, the bottom of our air mattress was sitting in a pool of water, our sleeping bags and pillows were wet, the walls and roof of our tent were sagging. We ran to our friends' tent next to us (who, by the way, had a tent as dry as a bone) and snuggled in. As we all lay there watching the lightning streak across the sky, we began to question the safety of our little refuge. So, off we scrambled to the car, which at least had four rubber tires to ground out any stray lightning bolts. Feeling a bit safer, we tried to get comfy and settle in for the night. That, unfortunately, proved to be a struggle. We had managed to get out of the rain but now became unbearably hot as we couldn't open our windows to allow in any moving air. Soon after that, and adding to our little world of misery, we began to hear the quiet buzzing of mosquitoes circling overhead, knowing we were their helpless prey. One by one, random slaps began to echo throughout the car, along with sighs, groans, and silent utterings of all kinds. I believe some of mine were variations of "I hate camping!

It is SO time to go home! I hate mosquitoes! Why in the world did God create such horrid insects?" The morning finally came, and we emerged from the car—a little sore, a little bit up, very tired, but alive. Needless to say, we left our little spot of paradise for home very soon following that night. We had survived our first camping experience and our last.

I praise the Lord that tents aren't permanent dwellings. Even if you love to tent camp for the weekend, your back may grow a little sore from sleeping on the ground, you may get weary securing your food from the wildlife and keeping your kids out of the poison ivy. You may become a little more irritable just because there comes a point when you've had enough and you just want to go home.

I had the privilege of working as a chaplain at a local continuing-care retirement community where I visited, prayed with, and led Bible studies for senior citizens. Daily, I would "sit at the feet" of people who had experienced seventy, eighty, and ninety years of life and learn vital lessons. I was gleaning from them in my thirties what they had learned in their fifties, sixties, and beyond. I can already say with boldness, it will be one of the highlights of my life. I learned life lessons like:

- Three keys to living a joyful and victorious life: Jesus Christ, a positive attitude, and a thankful heart. We have a choice when life throws the tough stuff at us. We can choose to keep our eyes on these and rise above the situation, or we can choose to keep our

eyes on ourselves and become negative and bitter.

- Relationships are what matter in life. The time and investment we make in others determine the dividends we receive later.

- Life isn't fair no matter what our age and stage of life because we live in a broken world.

- Our faith in Jesus is all that remains when life has stripped us of what the earth deems valuable.

- Healing can sometimes come slowly, but with every trace of it we can be assured we're headed in the right direction.

- We naturally assign ourselves value by what we do, not by who (or whose) we are. And because of it, we struggle when change occurs.

- To grow older can be difficult, but to grow older with Jesus is beautiful. Our bodies will deteriorate, but inwardly we are being renewed every day (2 Corinthians 4:16).

I sat across from numerous people who were dealing with one, if not all, of the above lessons. But every single one of them knew what it was like to go camping. Perhaps they didn't go to a campground like I had, but they had been living in "tents" for quite some time. Their bodies weren't working like they once did, and health problems emerged. Their thinking slowed, and memories came with more difficulty. Growing weary and uncomfortable, they

came to the point where they just wanted to go home to be with Jesus. Every single one of them had learned that no matter how diligently they had tried to beautify, care for, and nourish their bodies, they continued to change and "waste away" (2 Corinthians 4:16). Some at different rates, of course, due to heredity or the way they cared for themselves, but nonetheless, there was inevitable change. Talking to numerous people over several years, I had incredible discussions about this life and the next.

In many of those discussions, I had the privilege of asking lots of questions to those who have "been there, done that"—and women and the struggle with body image was no exception. My very kind and wonderfully humored ninety-one-year-old girlfriend shared with me that when she was growing up she was very paranoid about her string-bean but busty figure. She was always a head taller than everyone in the class through elementary and high school and therefore, stood out. She absolutely hated it. But she began to accept herself for who God made her to be when she took her eyes off herself and put them on others. She found her passion in various interests and with the Lord's help discovered contentment. She admits culture wasn't as obnoxious as it is today with images constantly in front of her, but girls did deal with the pressures of "fitting in." As proved before, her mother was instrumental in her perception of herself. She served as her continual source of affirmation, consistently affirming her as God's beautiful girl and helping her to refocus on the beauty of her character.

When I asked her what her words of wisdom to today's woman would be, she said, "Quit worrying about those things you don't like about yourself, unless it is affecting your health. Pray, put your thoughts and energies into something worthwhile, take your eyes off yourself, and begin to help others. Don't obsess over your body. The Lord looks at our soul, not our size. I still have big boobs, but I don't dwell on it. There is no use. Be content, take care of yourself, exercise, and do what you're able to do."

Another friend in her eighties, one of the wisest women in the world to me, also struggled with beauty and image. She had a similar stature but talked more about fashion—and remembers this story like it was yesterday. She was very poor and only owned two dresses that were made from grain sacks. Her parents couldn't afford to buy her shoes so a kind friend took the liberty to do so. As she entered school one day, already embarrassed because of her situation, one of the "well-to-do" girls made fun of her. This one mocking comment stayed with her for a lifetime. Fortunately, she too had a source of consistent encouragement in her life: a teacher who saw her for the way God gifted her and spoke truth to her. Her advice to us? "Turn your eyes. Turn your eyes from the lies of images to the truth of God's Word. To struggle doesn't do any good." She quoted Psalm 30:11 (NIV), which says, "You [God] turned my wailing into dancing; you removed my sackcloth and clothed me with joy." Talk about the Word of God speaking directly to her situation! But it speaks to you and me as well. When we

turn our eyes to Jesus, when we soak in His declaration of who He is and who we are because of Him, the lies give way to truth and our discontentment becomes celebration! Keep looking up.

Both of these women have lived much of life and have struggled like you and I have. The perspective, the disappointments, the dissatisfaction we can have in regard to ourselves and our bodies has been around for a long time. But the bigger picture involves looking at our bodies with an eternal perspective. These women have learned what's important and what's not. They have learned what is worth investing in and what isn't. They have discovered that because of Jesus, they don't need culture's approval. They know these bodies are earthly, temporary, and are going to give out. They have learned to turn their eyes from deceptive traps and lift them to heaven. They can testify that their bodies have been fearfully and wonderfully made and have served Jesus in glorifying ways, but because of a broken world they aren't the type that will last. However, because of Jesus, we have the opportunity to receive one that will. No weaknesses, no illnesses, no allergies, no injuries, no limitations. No flaws, no imperfections, no acne, no wrinkles, no leg cellulite, no stretch marks, and absolutely no rolls. There will no longer be any dissatisfaction when you look in the mirror. There will no longer be a skewed perspective. We won't have to search for the whole picture anymore, or believe only with our hearts that it is there. Because we will see it—the whole picture will be unveiled and revealed. And you will enjoy every bit of it! Because of the Holy Spirit—the Spirit of God, which is available through a relationship with Jesus Christ—our bodies will be powerfully transformed when Jesus comes again (Romans 8:11). It will be a body that will love perfectly, serve perfectly, desire perfectly, see perfectly, look perfect, feel perfect, and be perfect in every way possible. It will be a body of glorious and beautiful splendor. It will be what the Bible calls our resurrection body. Our earthly bodies are made fearfully and wonderfully and are exposed to the conditions of a broken world. Can you imagine how magnificent our resurrection bodies will be living in perfection?

I want you to read this next section of scripture out loud and soak it in. Paul, the author of 1 Corinthians, writes about our resurrection bodies, trying to compare the transformation to something we can get our finite minds around. But as anything else pertaining to God, it will far exceed our capability and imagination.

*Some skeptic is sure to ask, "Show me how resurrection works. Give me a diagram; draw me a picture. What does this 'resurrection body' look like?" If you look at this question closely, you realize how absurd it is. There are no diagrams for this kind of thing. We do have a parallel experience in gardening. You plant a "dead" seed; soon there is a flourishing plant. There is no visual likeness between seed and plant. You could never guess what a tomato would look like*

by looking at a tomato seed. What we plant in the soil and what grows out of it don't look anything alike. The dead body that we bury in the ground and the resurrection body that comes from it will be dramatically different.

You will notice that the variety of bodies is stunning. Just as there are different kinds of seeds, there are different kinds of bodies—humans, animals, birds, fish—each unprecedented in its form. You get a hint at the diversity of resurrection glory by looking at the diversity of bodies not only on earth but in the skies— sun, moon, stars—all these varieties of beauty and brightness. And we're only looking at pre-resurrection "seeds"—who can imagine what the resurrection "plants" will be like!

This image of planting a dead seed and raising a live plant is a mere sketch at best, but perhaps it will help in approaching the mystery of the resurrection body—but only if you keep in mind that when we're raised, we're raised for good, alive forever! The corpse that's planted is no beauty, but when it's raised, it's glorious. Put in the ground weak, it comes up powerful. The seed sown is natural; the seed grown is supernatural— same seed, same body, but what a difference from when it goes down in physical mortality to when it is raised up in spiritual immortality!

1 CORINTHIANS 15:35–44 (MSG)

I am definitely not a green thumb. Ask my family, I kill plants just by walking past them. But one year I decided I was going to hone my domestic skill of gardening and canning, and plant my first garden. I dug furrows, planted my little seeds, watered them over the next while, and then hoped for the best. So you can imagine the thrill of my heart weeks later, when I actually saw the evidence of green stems emerge from the ground. The day I saw new life I remember being in total awe of God, knowing it was only Him that could transform little reddish-brown seeds into something completely different—into something vibrantly colorful and food that would give us nourishment. He took the death of a seed and brought life from it! And so He can do with us.

Paul goes on to say in 1 Corinthians 15 that because of earth's first man, Adam, we are the way we are. We have physical, earthly bodies with individual personalities. Therefore, we think a certain way. We do things a certain way. Basically, we live to please ourselves. In and of ourselves, there is nothing good in us. We can't do it or get it right on our own—we're totally incapable, completely hopeless. Our hearts are selfish and sinful. The Bible calls us spiritually dead. And because of Adam, every single human is born like this. He and Eve turned from God way back when, and we received their spiritual DNA. But because of Jesus, God's Son, we have the opportunity for heart and life transformation. Because God loves us so much and doesn't want us separated from Him, He sent His Son Jesus to rescue us and bring our spirits back to

life. Jesus came to earth as a baby, grew to be a man, and died for you and me on a cross. He was God's Son, perfect in every way. He is the One who can get it right every time. On that cross He gave us His righteousness, His right standing before God, and took our sin upon Himself. He died, was buried, and three days later rose again by the power of the Holy Spirit, which lives in Him. And in doing so, He defeated the power of hell, Satan, and death. You and I don't have to face the punishment we deserve because Jesus faced it for us and won. You and I are set free, declared innocent from any guilt. The mistakes we have made, the people we have hurt, the wrong things we have done, have all been forgiven. As someone who has invited Jesus to be Lord of her life, believes what He has said, and has a relationship with Him, you have this same power, this same Holy Spirit living inside of you. You belong to heaven just like Jesus does, and you will be made like Him when He returns. The body you have now will be transformed into a resurrection body by the power of the Holy Spirit. Absolutely incredible! Paul concludes the chapter with a declaration of victory:

> *But let me tell you something wonderful, a*
> *mystery I'll probably never fully understand.*
> *We're not all going to die—but we are all going*
> *to be changed. You hear a blast to end all blasts*
> *from a trumpet, and in the time that you look*
> *up and blink your eyes—it's over. On signal*
> *from that trumpet from heaven, the dead will be*

*up and out of their graves, beyond the reach of death, never to die again. At the same moment and in the same way, we'll all be changed. In the resurrection scheme of things, this has to happen: everything perishable taken off the shelves and replaced by the imperishable, this mortal replaced by the immortal. Then the saying will come true:*

*Death swallowed by triumphant Life! Who got the last word, oh, Death? Oh, Death, who's afraid of you now?*

*It was sin that made death so frightening and law-code guilt that gave sin its leverage, its destructive power. But now in a single victorious stroke of Life, all three—sin, guilt, death—are gone, the gift of our Master, Jesus Christ. Thank God!* 1 CORINTHIANS 15: 51–57 (MSG)

The body you now possess will be changed and transformed into something perfect. It is already beautiful but will be made glorious. God has big plans for you and your body, now and for eternity! You will reign with Jesus, serve Him, and have wonderful things to do in running His kingdom. You will laugh, experience joy, peace, and the freedom that you've always longed for. Philippians 3:20–21 (NIV) promises, "And we eagerly await a Savior from there, the Lord Jesus Christ, who, by the power that enables him to bring everything under his control, will transform our lowly bodies so that they will be like his glorious body." Your body will be like the glorious one of

Jesus. You will finally be clothed with heaven.

> *That's why we live with such good cheer. You won't*
> *see us drooping our heads or dragging our feet!*
> *Cramped conditions here don't get us down. They*
> *only remind us of the spacious living conditions*
> *ahead. It's what we trust in but don't yet see that*
> *keeps us going. Do you suppose a few ruts in the*
> *road or rocks in the path are going to stop us?*
> *When the time comes, we'll be plenty ready to*
> *exchange exile for homecoming.*
> 2 Corinthians 5:6–8 (MSG)

I held her hand as she lay in bed, praying for the Lord to shower her with His peace and presence. My dear friend, well into her eighties, was dying. Her heart and life had revolved around her family, and she was anxious about leaving them. She had lost her husband, who she called "Dad," seven years earlier.

A week later, her daughter called me and said that her mother had gone home to be with the Lord earlier that morning. She said that they had experienced the most wonderful gift prior to her mother taking her last breath. Her mother, who had been resting quietly with her eyes closed, suddenly opened them and said, "Dad . . .Dad. . .is this heaven? Is this heaven? I wanna die! I wanna die!" And with those words, she slipped away from this world and into the next. After focusing on her family her entire life, it took one glance of heaven to thrill

her heart and race for home. She left her family behind and embraced Jesus. Her tent came down, was folded up, and she received her new body, one far more spectacular. She was able to finally leave the campground and head for the mansion.

# DISCUSSION QUESTIONS

1. From your own personal experience, how can you relate camping to living in your earthly body?

2. Leviticus 19:32 (NIV) says, "Stand up in the presence of the aged, show respect for the elderly and revere your God. I am the LORD." Considering the Lord's perspective of those who are older, how will this change how seriously you listen to and embrace the wisdom they have to share?

3. Reading the life lessons shared, which one resonates with you?

4. What is one thing you can glean from the two senior ladies who have "been there, done that"?

5. How does the scripture from 1 Corinthians 15 speak to you?

6. How does viewing your body with an eternal perspective continue to broaden the picture for you?

# Notes

# Notes

# Notes

# Notes

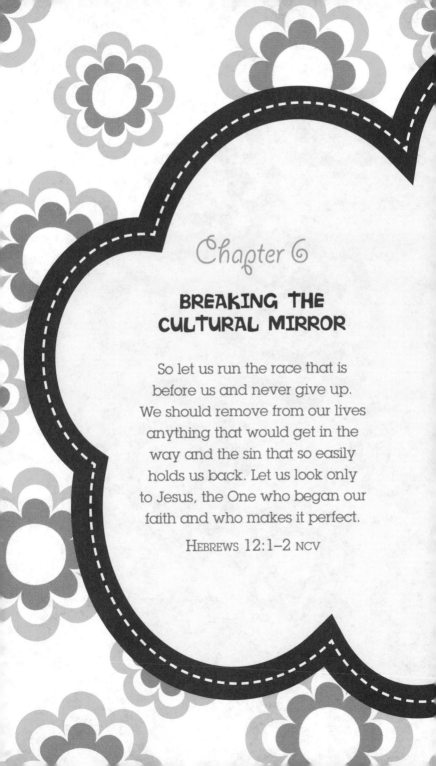

*Chapter 6*

## BREAKING THE
## CULTURAL MIRROR

So let us run the race that is before us and never give up. We should remove from our lives anything that would get in the way and the sin that so easily holds us back. Let us look only to Jesus, the One who began our faith and who makes it perfect.

HEBREWS 12:1–2 NCV

> God loves us the way we are
> but He loves us too much
> to leave us that way.
>
> LEIGHTON FORD

We identify lies by learning truth. And we not only learn truth, but we take one step further, and believe it. It's like jumping off the diving board and plunging into the depths of the water below—soaking ourselves from head to toe. The difference between knowing and growing is obedience. The difference between knowing and believing is living it out. But that seems to be where we fall short every time because things can get in our way. The lies we believe about ourselves, the lies we've believed about God, the skewed perspectives of others we've adopted, the sins that can so easily trip us up, our self-focused desires all fight to remain in control of our hearts.

But interestingly, the Bible mentions repeatedly the relationship between our hearts and our eyes (Psalm

101:2–3; 119:36–37). It even mentions the eyes of our hearts (Ephesians 1:18), meaning our understanding or inner awareness.[22] Matthew 6:21–23 (NCV) speaks of the focus of our hearts and follows with, "The eye is a light for the body. If your eyes are good, your whole body will be full of light. But if your eyes are evil, your whole body will be full of darkness." Whether we speak of the eyes in our head or the eyes of our hearts, our eyes serve as a gate. They have the power to allow or keep out what goes into our minds and hearts.

Many of us may know truth, but our hearts haven't embraced it. We may speak it, but it isn't reflected in our thinking or actions. Our vision has shifted from Jesus to what He can give us, then over to others, then back to ourselves, and everywhere in between. Our hearts become saturated in discontent and ingratitude rather than in the joy of His presence and being cared for. One huge distraction and lie along the way that we fall prey to is the trap of comparisons. We look at others, longing for them to fill our cup of emotional need and affirmation. We grow jealous, discontented, or adopt a "less than" mentality about ourselves. We aren't as good as what or who we see. We may desire their personalities, their bodies, their talents, their wealth, their husbands, their spiritual giftings, or even their seemingly "all-together" lives.

With comparisons come bizarre thoughts and behaviors. For example, a friend of mine shared a story

---

22. *The NIV Study Bible* (Grand Rapids, MI: Zondervan, 1985).

with me about her and a friend comparing chest sizes. All in good humor, they debated which of them boasted the largest and most gravity-enhanced bustline. One of them grabbed a stapler and, fully clothed, proceeded to place it under her breast to show that it hung low enough to hold the stapler in place. My friend then grabbed a rolled-up newspaper and put it under her breast. Wanting bragging rights, her competitor grabbed a phone book, which sent my friend running for a jar of pickles, which by the way, worked. The pickles only encouraged the other to seize a can of pop until the competition escalated even further. The final item grabbed was a prepackaged Duraflame log. This turned into a failed attempt causing great disappointment. These two grown women, each married with children, stood in the kitchen comparing and competing, laughing at themselves, wondering what in the world their kids would say if they walked in and saw them.

As funny and as good humored as that story is, the thoughts and behaviors that can come with comparisons are not. When we compare ourselves to others, we are treading on dangerous and destructive ground. I have learned that comparison thinking can lead me to think and do things that are not based in truth, things that may appear so real to me but to outsiders looking in, seem obviously "silly" and bizarre. Comparisons in my life have produced blackened spots on my heart—spots of jealousy, resentment, and ingratitude. I'm sad to say there have been numerous times when I've missed the joys and adventure God had for me. There have been times I neglected to see God's handprints as He worked in or around me. I have sacrificed opportunities to love others well, showing them who Jesus is. I have the opportunity of a lifetime to know, serve, and worship God joyfully and intimately, but when I live in "Comparison Campground" I trade those privileges for elusive peace and unfulfilled satisfaction. To look at others consistently in comparison, to look "horizontal" at seemingly greener grass, will hold us back. Imagine all that we *could* be if we would embrace who He has made us to be! Our gaze on others grieves God and communicates to our Creator that in our eyes His work isn't good enough. That what He has given us isn't good enough, and in essence, that He can't deliver. Lies are destructive, but lies pertaining to God's character blind us to everything else.

Melinda Doolittle, singer and author, speaks a wise word to those who catch themselves comparing and competing with others:

> To me, that passage [Psalm 139:13–16] says that we matter to God: He made us, and even before we were born, He established a plan for our lives. We cannot base our estimation of ourselves on the fickle opinions of other people. That's why I believe I am only in competition with myself. Certainly, I want to be the best "me" possible, so I work at my craft. I try to take good care of my body, mind, and spirit. But I don't base my self-

*esteem on someone else's idea of who I should be. Funny, many images of celebrities or models in magazines nowadays are "computer enhanced," altered to look better by someone who is handy with a mouse. The images themselves are not even real, much less valid comparisons. So rather than comparing yourself to anyone else, simply relax and enjoy being the person God made you to be. You are your own competition. In fact, you are your only competition.*[23]

One thing God is teaching me is that it's imperative that I keep my gaze "vertical," not just for the length of a chapter like we strived to do in chapter two, but for a lifetime. It's time for a lifestyle of looking to Him rather than looking around. After all, who do I want to look like more, the girl down the street or increasingly more like my Savior, Jesus Christ? Where our eyes are fixed, our hearts and feet will follow. If we fix our eyes on people, we will follow hard after them. We will lean toward their values and choices. But if we fix our eyes on Christ, we will follow hard after *Him*. One leads to bondage, the other to freedom. Today and every day, moment by moment, we can choose Him.

Others of us may have tried looking at God because we have heard about His heart for us, but He wasn't what we needed Him to be. Our lives were hellish, people let

23. Melinda Doolittle, "Chucking the Comparisons," *Words of Life*, accessed February, 14, 2010, http://lifetoday.org/connect/words-of-life/chucking-the-comparisons.

us down, and God wasn't there. We felt rejected and hurt, so we have guarded our hearts and minds with shields of self-protective armor ever since. We believe there is no one who can love us the way we need to be loved, especially not God. So our eyes have been focused on our self-sufficiency and ourselves. And we feel lonely, angry, unfulfilled, and hopeless.

The way we feel about our bodies goes a whole lot deeper than if we have flabby arms or a big nose. This doesn't include issues only about body image but other issues as well: self-protection, self-striving, perfectionism, an identity that is performance or approval based, issues with control, or any other heart issue that we deal with—the source is all the same. We haven't known perfect love. Nobody is capable of giving it, including us, which also means we have never received it. I can only speak from experience here. For most of my life, I set the bar so high for myself to succeed in everything that my goals weren't even realistic. I was an approval addict and people pleaser. I was competitive and jealous, constantly comparing myself to others. I was critical and condemning of others but hardest on myself. Failure was not an option. Perfection was the standard. So, no matter what I accomplished or how worthy of celebration my achievement was, it still fell short and wasn't good enough for me. Self-striving and self-works became a way of life. It impacted the way I saw and did everything in life, even my perspective of my salvation. Until finally one day God revealed to me that fear was what was driving me, and He spoke 1 John 4:15–19 (MSG) to me in a fresh new way:

> *Everyone who confesses that Jesus is God's*
> *Son participates continuously in an intimate*
> *relationship with God. We know it so well,*
> *we've embraced it heart and soul, this love that*
> *comes from God. God is love. When we take up*
> *permanent residence in a life of love, we live in*
> *God and God lives in us. This way, love has the*
> *run of the house, becomes at home and mature*
> *in us, so that we're free of worry on Judgment*
> *Day—our standing in the world is identical with*
> *Christ's. There is no room in love for fear. Well-*
> *formed love banishes fear. Since fear is crippling,*
> *a fearful life—fear of death, fear of judgment—is*
> *one not yet fully formed in love. We, though, are*
> *going to love—love and be loved. First we were*
> *loved, now we love. He loved us first.*

Jesus loves us perfectly. There are no cracks, flaws, or shortcomings in His love. We don't have to work, strive, perform, or earn His love but can rest there. I am hidden in, covered by, saturated with, and soaking in His perfect, complete, unfailing, unconditional, unyielding, lavish love. In Him, we don't have to fear failure, insignificance, or rejection. The Bible is filled with truth He has spoken about you and me, but it is up to us if we will choose to believe it and walk in it. And if we struggle with believing it, we can ask Him to help us believe it (Mark 9:14–24)!

We have been declared perfect as God continues to make us more like Him (Hebrews 10:14). Scripture says that God has set His affections on us, called us His treasured possession and the apple of His eye (Deuteronomy 7:6–7; Zechariah 2:8). God says He is enthralled with our beauty (Psalm 45:11) and in fact says we have captured His heart (Song of Songs 4:9). God is passionate about us. And it's all because of Jesus. We are sinners in need of a Savior. The things we have done wrong, the bad thoughts we have entertained, the poor choices we have made, Jesus took away when He died on the cross. He declared us innocent. And because Jesus paid the price we should have paid, we can spend forever with Him. With His arms open wide while nailed to the cross, He called us valued, chosen, and forgiven, and said to us, "I'd rather die than to live without you." He is asking each one of us to put our trust in Him and become His child. We don't have to do it alone anymore. We don't have to fear anymore. We can begin a new life today, one that will last forever with Him. As we believe and embrace His perfect love and live in it, we can love others and even ourselves in a whole new way. We can finally live in His peace and joy in who He made us to be.

No matter where our eyes have focused in the past, we can choose differently today. We can turn our eyes to Jesus and refuse to take them off Him. Those who do this battle in this broken world, refuting the lies that pound on the door of their hearts and minds. Instead of falling prey to the lies, they choose to fall into the depths of God's loving truth and believe it—and it's written all over their lives. Jesus came to do the will of His Father. Like Jesus, we can focus resolutely on the joy that lies in front of us, no matter how hard the battle. We know that nothing we walk through will ever be more difficult than what Jesus had to face and endure. As He stumbled to the cross, perhaps the joy that Jesus focused on was the day when He would finally see what His death accomplished as He gazed at all those in heaven with Him. Perhaps the joy Jesus kept in front of Him was your face and mine. But in my mind, the joy and desire that Jesus kept in front of Him was His Father and knowing He was walking in the desires of His Father's heart.

God loves us perfectly, longs to save us from hell and ourselves, but wants something more. One of the desires of His heart is intimacy with us—a close, familiar, loving, personal relationship. It isn't just a conversation here or there, praying only when we need Him to come through for us or before dinner. Intimacy is *living* in relationship with Him—day by day, moment by moment. I know that I have only scratched the surface of intimacy in my relationship with Jesus because intimacy with Him is limitless. But I can trust Him to show me, teach me, and take me deeper with Him. He has shown me that His children can experience intimacy with Him, from laughing with Him throughout the day, to talking to Him about anything on our hearts and minds. We can ask Him for help in the fun little things of life from picking out an outfit to picking the right gift. We can cry out to

Him in the heart-wrenching things of life just because we're hurting or angry or when we don't understand what in the world is going on. He wants to talk to us through His Word, listen to us as we pour out our hearts, thrill us, surprise us, teach us, protect us, comfort us, and love us the way we need to be loved. He wants our eyes on Him. He wants our hearts, our ears, our obedience, our love, our trust, our adoration, and our praise. He wants every inch of us. He knows our hearts are searching and longing to be filled with acceptance, approval, security, significance, and love. And He watches us run to many different sources to find them. But He also knows He is the only One that can satisfy, and He wants to bless us with Himself, and for us to seek or believe anything else grieves Him. Jesus wants us to see His heart, to see Him for who He really is, not who we have made Him to be in our minds or how we have pictured Him because of our pained earthly relationships.

Several years ago, I was sitting in my living room discouraged. My prayers felt as though they bounced off the ceiling, and I felt very much alone. I told the Lord how I was feeling and asked Him if He was there. After several minutes of sharing my heart, something caught my eye. Right outside my window on the sill sat a bright, beautiful cardinal. He sat there for some time and didn't fly away. I felt the Lord saying to me, "I am here. You are not alone. The earth is full of My glory." I have always delighted in creation—sunrises, rainbows, waterfalls, flowers—because it reflects the Father's creativity and beauty. And perhaps more than I should, I take it very personally. Not only does it reflect Him, but He put it here for me to enjoy, so I do. But God took a little red cardinal that He fashioned and used it to declare His love for me. After that time, I saw cardinals everywhere. I was reminded again and again that the earth is full of Him, that life may be difficult at times, but He is always there. I tell you that story from years ago to tell you this: God's Spirit continues to speak to us through His Word, through His people, through circumstances, and He continues to use His creation. I was driving the other day, crying and feeling anxious about the day ahead, when a beautiful cardinal glided across my path in front of my van. God has done that numerous times for me. And every time, the truth speaks as loudly as the first time I heard it. Instantly, I am reminded that I have nothing to fear, nothing to be anxious about. God's Spirit is with us, and He loves us so much. And the fact that He would be kind and sweet enough to take what He knows to get our attention, and use it to lift our eyes, reflects His heart for us. Intimacy. He initiates it all the time. And He has His own love language for each of us. As precious as it feels to be held by God, intimacy with Him isn't just a feeling, nor is it just in a moment, but it increases as we walk toward Him and *live* in the desires of His heart. That's where He wants us. To walk in what He desires isn't always easiest, but to walk there is the most rewarding, the most fulfilling, the most growing, and the most peaceful.

Jesus not only wants us to see Him, but to trust Him with all that we have and with all that we are. Intimacy is surrendering every single part of us to Him so He can grow us to look more like Him—seeing with His eyes, loving with His love, walking in His will, and being obedient in what He has called us to do. It is realizing we don't have to perform, but that He is doing the work in and through us. Jesus said our job is to join with Him and live there: "I am the Vine, you are the branches. When you're joined with me and I with you, the relation intimate and organic, the harvest is sure to be abundant. Separated, you can't produce a thing" (John 15:5 MSG). He goes on to say, "I've loved you the way my Father has loved me. Make yourselves at home in my love. If you keep my commands, you'll remain intimately at home in my love. That's what I've done—kept my Father's commands and made myself at home in his love" (John 15:9–10 MSG). Jesus had spiritual intimacy with His Father because He lived in His Father's love, living out what His Father had called Him to do and trusted Him every step of the way. We also have His words, His truths, and His perfect love to live, rest, and persevere in not only when life is hard but all the time. It's time to accept His invitation and make ourselves at home. We're not talking a casual stop in for coffee and dessert; we're talking about unpacking our bags and staying. Because of who He is, we can abandon fear and trust Him radically. He asks us to be faithful where He has placed us, and in the little things He has given us to do for that day. He has given every single one of us the Gospel and a gift to use to give His grace to this world (1 Peter 4:10). Are we using it? Are we investing it for Him to multiply? Or have we become so distracted by our culture, or even by our very own selves, that we have buried it (Matthew 25:14–30)? Our Father and walking in the desires of His heart: that is our joy. That is our focus.

If everything about us is pointing to Jesus, we are walking in His truth and love, and doing what He has called us to do, we can see why our enemy is throwing distractions at us in hopes to divert our eyes and hearts. It is imperative we become alert and aware. So, it's time to get countercultural. "As you come to him, the living Stone—rejected by humans but chosen by God and precious to him—you also, like living stones, are being built into a spiritual house to be a holy priesthood" (1 Peter 2:4–5 NIV). The Bible describes Jesus as the Living Stone and He is building us into a spiritual house with Himself as our foundation and strength. It's time to take our Stone and break the cultural mirror we've been using to size ourselves up. We've been given a new mirror to gaze into—one that reflects the true picture.

Is there work to be done? You bet. There may be things in our lives that are holding us back and weighing us down, things we need to choose to take care of and put an end to. Bringing those to Him, we can trust that He will walk with us every step of the way, giving us wisdom, strength, courage, and grace to learn and grow in our perceptions, thinking, lifestyle habits, and our faith.

This new mirror He has hung in front of us no longer reflects our imperfections in the world's light, but our beauty in a heavenly one. Because our new mirror doesn't just reflect *our* image anymore; it reflects His. Next time you make that infamous turn, enjoy your new perspective.

> But you are the ones chosen by God, chosen for the high calling of priestly work, chosen to be a holy people, God's instruments to do his work and speak out for him, to tell others of the night-and-day difference he made for you—from nothing to something, from rejected to accepted.
>
> 1 PETER 2:9–10 (MSG)

You, my dear, have a higher calling. Now go, and live it out.

*Lord, I come and give myself to You as an offering. Take every part of me—from the top of my head to the soles of my feet, from the innermost parts to the outermost parts. Take the best of me and the rest of me. Take my heart, because I can't do it on my own. I am a sinner saved only by Your grace. Apart from You, there is nothing good or beautiful in me. Holy Spirit, come into my heart and begin to move, begin to uncover the lies that are buried there about who You are—Your character and Your heart—about who I am, how I see myself, about my body, and my relationship with You. Reveal Yourself and the truths You want me to discover about who You made me to be. Give me the desire and the strength to take steps to walk in that privilege. Show me what real and intimate relationship with You is like. I want to walk in the desires of Your heart. Amen.*

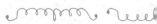

# DISCUSSION QUESTIONS

1.  Which scenario best describes where your focus and heart have been? Share a little about your experience.

    a.  Focusing back and forth between Jesus and other things/knowing truth but having difficulty embracing it

    b.  Focusing on yourself and your sufficiency/not even claiming to believe truth

    c.  Consistently focusing on Jesus/knowing and believing truth and living it out

2.  Do you struggle with comparisons? How has that affected your heart, your relationships, your life, your perspective of God?

3.  As you look at your life up to this point, have you tasted perfect love in your relationship with Jesus? His Holy Spirit works in our hearts and reveals this perfect love to us, but what are steps we can take to be open to experiencing this love?

4.  What does intimacy with God look like to you?

5.  How would keeping our focus on "walking in the desires of God's heart" change our overall perspective, our hearts, our intimacy with God, our relationships with others, our lives?

6. What does it mean for you personally to shatter the cultural mirror?

7. What things are holding you back that you need to remove from your life?

8. How has the Holy Spirit spoken to you while reading this book?

9. The difference between knowing and growing is obedience. The difference between knowing and believing is living it out. How will you apply what the Spirit has spoken to you?

10. We can hear God's voice and discover His heart in various ways, but primarily through His Word. To foster intimacy and nurture your relationship with God, how can you make reading His Word part of your day? What are some creative ways you can spend time with and enjoy Him?

# Notes

........................................................................

........................................................................

........................................................................

........................................................................

........................................................................

........................................................................

........................................................................

........................................................................

........................................................................

........................................................................

........................................................................

........................................................................

........................................................................

........................................................................

# Notes

# Notes

........................................................
........................................................
........................................................
........................................................
........................................................
........................................................
........................................................
........................................................
........................................................
........................................................
........................................................
........................................................
........................................................
........................................................

# Notes

# Conclusion

I will never forget the morning I stopped at the bank to get some money. The bank was closed so I conveniently used the ATM. I had retrieved the money and climbed back into my van where my boys were patiently waiting. I had driven in the wrong way, so I thought I would turn my van around and leave through the appropriate drive. As I backed up, I heard a loud bang. I looked in my rearview mirror, and there I saw the lamppost, seemingly in slow motion, falling back toward the bank wall. I slammed the gearshift into PARK and jumped out of my van. The lamppost was leaning against the wall and hanging by a thread to its base. So I did what any sensible person would do—I tried to reconnect it. I lugged that post up in the air and assessed the situation, angling it this way and that, hoping by some miraculous act of God it would just pop into place. As this "brainiac" woman was trying desperately to fix her error, a car drove up and out came the biggest, burliest, bearded man I ever saw. As I began to try to explain what happened, he took the post and in a mere five seconds laid it down and got back into his car. That was my sign that there was no fixing this lamp. So I got back into my van, knowing I needed to make the dreaded phone call to the bank and admit my faux pas.

As I drove down the road toward home, my youngest son, Cade, said, "Well Mom, look at the bright side." Looking for any redeeming quality regarding what just happened, I said, "Oh yeah? What's that?" With his characteristic ornery grin, he said, "Oh wait. There is no bright side." And with that, we all began to laugh. I had lost focus, and it caused some damage. My loss of focus didn't just affect me, but if affected others as well.

It's the same with truth. Our focus affects others. My friend shared with me that some of the best gifts she ever received were sealed envelopes from her friends. Inside were written letters for her, expressing their love and appreciation. On the "bad days" of life she was to open a letter to be reminded how much she was loved and to keep her focused on truth. God has done the same for you and me. In the Bible, He has written us a letter expressing to us His declaration of love and who we are in Him. And not only on the bad days, but every day, we can keep His truth in front of us to stay focused. Because with Jesus, there is always a bright side. And as we choose to receive and believe truth daily, we are then credible to pass this gift on to others—not just by what we say, but by the way we live. Let's keep it vertical, girlfriends!

> *Yes, all the things I once thought were so important are gone from my life. Compared to the high privilege of knowing Christ Jesus as my Master, firsthand, everything I once thought I had going for me is insignificant—dog dung. I've dumped it all in the trash so that I could embrace Christ and be embraced by him. . . .*

I'm not saying that I have this all together, that I have it made. But I am well on my way, reaching out for Christ, who has so wondrously reached out for me. Friends, don't get me wrong: By no means do I count myself an expert in all of this, but I've got my eye on the goal, where God is beckoning us onward—to Jesus. I'm off and running, and I'm not turning back.

So let's keep focused on that goal, those of us who want everything God has for us. If any of you have something else in mind, something less than total commitment, God will clear your blurred vision—you'll see it yet! Now that we're on the right track, let's stay on it.

Stick with me, friends. Keep track of those you see running this same course, headed for this same goal. There are many out there taking other paths, choosing other goals, and trying to get you to go along with them. . . . All they want is easy street. They hate Christ's Cross. But easy street is a dead-end street. Those who live there make their bellies their gods; belches are their praise; all they can think of is their appetites.

But there's far more to life for us. We're citizens of high heaven! We're waiting the arrival of the Savior, the Master, Jesus Christ, who will transform our earthly bodies into glorious bodies like his own. He'll make us beautiful and whole with the same powerful skill by which he

*is putting everything as it should be, under and around him.*

*My dear, dear friends! I love you so much. I do want the very best for you. You make me feel such joy, fill me with such pride. Don't waver. Stay on track, steady in God.* PHILIPPIANS 3:7–9, 12–4:1 (MSG)

## About the Author

Jocelyn Hamsher serves as vice president of Circle of Friends Ministries. She is a speaker and author of *Meet Me at the Well Bible Study*, and a contributing author to *Shared Blessings* and *Shared Hope*, Circle of Friends' Devotionals. She and her husband, Bruce, have three sons and live in Sugarcreek, Ohio.

# What Is Circle of Friends?

Circle of Friends Ministries, Inc., is a nonprofit organization established to build a pathway for women to come into a personal relationship with Jesus Christ and to build Christian unity among women. Our mission is to honor Jesus Christ through meeting the needs of women in our local, national, and international communities. Our vision is to be women who are committed to Jesus Christ, obediently seeking God's will and fulfilling our life mission as Christ followers. As individuals and as a corporate group, we minister a Christ-centered hope, biblically based encouragement, and unconditional love by offering God-honoring, Word-based teaching, worship, accountability, and fellowship to women in a nondenominational environment through speaker services, worship teams, daily weblogs and devotionals, radio programs, and GirlFriends teen events.

COF also partners with churches and women's groups to bring conferences, retreats, Bible studies, concerts, simulcasts, and servant evangelism projects to their communities. We have a Marketplace Ministry that teaches kingdom principles in the workplace and are committed to undergirding, with prayer and financial support, foreign mission projects that impact the world for Jesus Christ. Our goal is to evangelize the lost and edify the body of Christ by touching the lives of women—locally, nationally, and globally. For more information, visit www.ourcircleoffriends.org.

# Read Thru the Bible in a Year

| | | | |
|---|---|---|---|
| 1-Jan | Gen. 1-2 | Matt. 1 | Ps. 1 |
| 2-Jan | Gen. 3-4 | Matt. 2 | Ps. 2 |
| 3-Jan | Gen. 5-7 | Matt. 3 | Ps. 3 |
| 4-Jan | Gen. 8-10 | Matt. 4 | Ps. 4 |
| 5-Jan | Gen. 11-13 | Matt. 5:1-20 | Ps. 5 |
| 6-Jan | Gen. 14-16 | Matt. 5:21-48 | Ps. 6 |
| 7-Jan | Gen. 17-18 | Matt. 6:1-18 | Ps. 7 |
| 8-Jan | Gen. 19-20 | Matt. 6:19-34 | Ps. 8 |
| 9-Jan | Gen. 21-23 | Matt. 7:1-11 | Ps. 9:1-8 |
| 10-Jan | Gen. 24 | Matt. 7:12-29 | Ps. 9:9-20 |
| 11-Jan | Gen. 25-26 | Matt. 8:1-17 | Ps. 10:1-11 |
| 12-Jan | Gen. 27:1-28:9 | Matt. 8:18-34 | Ps. 10:12-18 |
| 13-Jan | Gen. 28:10-29:35 | Matt. 9 | Ps. 11 |
| 14-Jan | Gen. 30:1-31:21 | Matt. 10:1-15 | Ps. 12 |
| 15-Jan | Gen. 31:22-32:21 | Matt. 10:16-36 | Ps. 13 |
| 16-Jan | Gen. 32:22-34:31 | Matt. 10:37-11:6 | Ps. 14 |
| 17-Jan | Gen. 35-36 | Matt. 11:7-24 | Ps. 15 |
| 18-Jan | Gen. 37-38 | Matt. 11:25-30 | Ps. 16 |
| 19-Jan | Gen. 39-40 | Matt. 12:1-29 | Ps. 17 |
| 20-Jan | Gen. 41 | Matt. 12:30-50 | Ps. 18:1-15 |
| 21-Jan | Gen. 42-43 | Matt. 13:1-9 | Ps. 18:16-29 |
| 22-Jan | Gen. 44-45 | Matt. 13:10-23 | Ps. 18:30-50 |
| 23-Jan | Gen. 46:1-47:26 | Matt. 13:24-43 | Ps. 19 |
| 24-Jan | Gen. 47:27-49:28 | Matt. 13:44-58 | Ps. 20 |
| 25-Jan | Gen. 49:29-Exod. 1:22 | Matt. 14 | Ps. 21 |
| 26-Jan | Exod. 2-3 | Matt. 15:1-28 | Ps. 22:1-21 |
| 27-Jan | Exod. 4:1-5:21 | Matt. 15:29-16:12 | Ps. 22:22-31 |
| 28-Jan | Exod. 5:22-7:24 | Matt. 16:13-28 | Ps. 23 |
| 29-Jan | Exod. 7:25-9:35 | Matt. 17:1-9 | Ps. 24 |
| 30-Jan | Exod. 10-11 | Matt. 17:10-27 | Ps. 25 |
| 31-Jan | Exod. 12 | Matt. 18:1-20 | Ps. 26 |
| 1-Feb | Exod. 13-14 | Matt. 18:21-35 | Ps. 27 |
| 2-Feb | Exod. 15-16 | Matt. 19:1-15 | Ps. 28 |
| 3-Feb | Exod. 17-19 | Matt. 19:16-30 | Ps. 29 |
| 4-Feb | Exod. 20-21 | Matt. 20:1-19 | Ps. 30 |
| 5-Feb | Exod. 22-23 | Matt. 20:20-34 | Ps. 31:1-8 |
| 6-Feb | Exod. 24-25 | Matt. 21:1-27 | Ps. 31:9-18 |
| 7-Feb | Exod 26-27 | Matt. 21:28-46 | Ps. 31:19-24 |
| 8-Feb | Exod. 28 | Matt. 22 | Ps. 32 |
| 9-Feb | Exod. 29 | Matt. 23:1-36 | Ps. 33:1-12 |
| 10-Feb | Exod. 30-31 | Matt. 23:37-24:28 | Ps. 33:13-22 |
| 11-Feb | Exod. 32-33 | Matt. 24:29-51 | Ps. 34:1-7 |

| | | | |
|---|---|---|---|
| 12-Feb | Exod. 34:1-35:29 | Matt. 25:1-13 | Ps. 34:8-22 |
| 13-Feb | Exod. 35:30-37:29 | Matt. 25:14-30 | Ps. 35:1-8 |
| 14-Feb | Exod. 38-39 | Matt. 25:31-46 | Ps. 35:9-17 |
| 15-Feb | Exod. 40 | Matt. 26:1-35 | Ps. 35:18-28 |
| 16-Feb | Lev. 1-3 | Matt. 26:36-68 | Ps. 36:1-6 |
| 17-Feb | Lev. 4:1-5:13 | Matt. 26:69-27:26 | Ps. 36:7-12 |
| 18-Feb | Lev. 5:14 -7:21 | Matt. 27:27-50 | Ps. 37:1-6 |
| 19-Feb | Lev. 7:22-8:36 | Matt. 27:51-66 | Ps. 37:7-26 |
| 20-Feb | Lev. 9-10 | Matt. 28 | Ps. 37:27-40 |
| 21-Feb | Lev. 11-12 | Mark 1:1-28 | Ps. 38 |
| 22-Feb | Lev. 13 | Mark 1:29-39 | Ps. 39 |
| 23-Feb | Lev. 14 | Mark 1:40-2:12 | Ps. 40:1-8 |
| 24-Feb | Lev. 15 | Mark 2:13-3:35 | Ps. 40:9-17 |
| 25-Feb | Lev. 16-17 | Mark 4:1-20 | Ps. 41:1-4 |
| 26-Feb | Lev. 18-19 | Mark 4:21-41 | Ps. 41:5-13 |
| 27-Feb | Lev. 20 | Mark 5 | Ps. 42-43 |
| 28-Feb | Lev. 21-22 | Mark 6:1-13 | Ps. 44 |
| 1-Mar | Lev. 23-24 | Mark 6:14-29 | Ps. 45:1-5 |
| 2-Mar | Lev. 25 | Mark 6:30-56 | Ps. 45:6-12 |
| 3-Mar | Lev. 26 | Mark 7 | Ps. 45:13-17 |
| 4-Mar | Lev. 27 | Mark 8 | Ps. 46 |
| 5-Mar | Num. 1-2 | Mark 9:1-13 | Ps. 47 |
| 6-Mar | Num. 3 | Mark 9:14-50 | Ps. 48:1-8 |
| 7-Mar | Num. 4 | Mark 10:1-34 | Ps. 48:9-14 |
| 8-Mar | Num. 5:1-6:21 | Mark 10:35-52 | Ps. 49:1-9 |
| 9-Mar | Num. 6:22-7:47 | Mark 11 | Ps. 49:10-20 |
| 10-Mar | Num. 7:48-8:4 | Mark 12:1-27 | Ps. 50:1-15 |
| 11-Mar | Num. 8:5-9:23 | Mark 12:28-44 | Ps. 50:16-23 |
| 12-Mar | Num. 10-11 | Mark 13:1-8 | Ps. 51:1-9 |
| 13-Mar | Num. 12-13 | Mark 13:9-37 | Ps. 51:10-19 |
| 14-Mar | Num. 14 | Mark 14:1-31 | Ps. 52 |
| 15-Mar | Num. 15 | Mark 14:32-72 | Ps. 53 |
| 16-Mar | Num. 16 | Mark 15:1-32 | Ps. 54 |
| 17-Mar | Num. 17-18 | Mark 15:33-47 | Ps. 55 |
| 18-Mar | Num. 19-20 | Mark 16 | Ps. 56:1-7 |
| 19-Mar | Num. 21:1-22:20 | Luke 1:1-25 | Ps. 56:8-13 |
| 20-Mar | Num. 22:21-23:30 | Luke 1:26-56 | Ps. 57 |
| 21-Mar | Num. 24-25 | Luke 1:57-2:20 | Ps. 58 |
| 22-Mar | Num. 26:1-27:11 | Luke 2:21-38 | Ps. 59:1-8 |
| 23-Mar | Num. 27:12-29:11 | Luke 2:39-52 | Ps. 59:9-17 |
| 24-Mar | Num. 29:12-30:16 | Luke 3 | Ps. 60:1-5 |
| 25-Mar | Num. 31 | Luke 4 | Ps. 60:6-12 |
| 26-Mar | Num. 32-33 | Luke 5:1-16 | Ps. 61 |
| 27-Mar | Num. 34-36 | Luke 5:17-32 | Ps. 62:1-6 |
| 28-Mar | Deut. 1:1-2:25 | Luke 5:33-6:11 | Ps. 62:7-12 |
| 29-Mar | Deut. 2:26-4:14 | Luke 6:12-35 | Ps. 63:1-5 |

| | | |
|---|---|---|
| 30-Mar | Deut. 4:15-5:22 | Luke 6:36-49 | Ps. 63:6-11 |
| 31-Mar | Deut. 5:23-7:26 | Luke 7:1-17 | Ps. 64:1-5 |
| 1-Apr | Deut. 8-9 | Luke 7:18-35 | Ps. 64:6-10 |
| 2-Apr | Deut. 10-11 | Luke 7:36-8:3 | Ps. 65:1-8 |
| 3-Apr | Deut. 12-13 | Luke 8:4-21 | Ps. 65:9-13 |
| 4-Apr | Deut. 14:1-16:8 | Luke 8:22-39 | Ps. 66:1-7 |
| 5-Apr | Deut. 16:9-18:22 | Luke 8:40-56 | Ps. 66:8-15 |
| 6-Apr | Deut. 19:1-21:9 | Luke 9:1-22 | Ps. 66:16-20 |
| 7-Apr | Deut. 21:10-23:8 | Luke 9:23-42 | Ps. 67 |
| 8-Apr | Deut. 23:9-25:19 | Luke 9:43-62 | Ps. 68:1-6 |
| 9-Apr | Deut. 26:1-28:14 | Luke 10:1-20 | Ps. 68:7-14 |
| 10-Apr | Deut. 28:15-68 | Luke 10:21-37 | Ps. 68:15-19 |
| 11-Apr | Deut. 29-30 | Luke 10:38-11:23 | Ps. 68:20-27 |
| 12-Apr | Deut. 31:1-32:22 | Luke 11:24-36 | Ps. 68:28-35 |
| 13-Apr | Deut. 32:23-33:29 | Luke 11:37-54 | Ps. 69:1-9 |
| 14-Apr | Deut. 34-Josh. 2 | Luke 12:1-15 | Ps. 69:10-17 |
| 15-Apr | Josh. 3:1-5:12 | Luke 12:16-40 | Ps. 69:18-28 |
| 16-Apr | Josh. 5:13-7:26 | Luke 12:41-48 | Ps. 69:29-36 |
| 17-Apr | Josh. 8-9 | Luke 12:49-59 | Ps. 70 |
| 18-Apr | Josh. 10:1-11:15 | Luke 13:1-21 | Ps. 71:1-6 |
| 19-Apr | Josh. 11:16-13:33 | Luke 13:22-35 | Ps. 71:7-16 |
| 20-Apr | Josh. 14-16 | Luke 14:1-15 | Ps. 71:17-21 |
| 21-Apr | Josh. 17:1-19:16 | Luke 14:16-35 | Ps. 71:22-24 |
| 22-Apr | Josh. 19:17-21:42 | Luke 15:1-10 | Ps. 72:1-11 |
| 23-Apr | Josh. 21:43-22:34 | Luke 15:11-32 | Ps. 72:12-20 |
| 24-Apr | Josh. 23-24 | Luke 16:1-18 | Ps. 73:1-9 |
| 25-Apr | Judg. 1-2 | Luke 16:19-17:10 | Ps. 73:10-20 |
| 26-Apr | Judg. 3-4 | Luke 17:11-37 | Ps. 73:21-28 |
| 27-Apr | Judg. 5:1-6:24 | Luke 18:1-17 | Ps. 74:1-3 |
| 28-Apr | Judg. 6:25-7:25 | Luke 18:18-43 | Ps. 74:4-11 |
| 29-Apr | Judg. 8:1-9:23 | Luke 19:1-28 | Ps. 74:12-17 |
| 30-Apr | Judg. 9:24-10:18 | Luke 19:29-48 | Ps. 74:18-23 |
| 1-May | Judg. 11:1-12:7 | Luke 20:1-26 | Ps. 75:1-7 |
| 2-May | Judg. 12:8-14:20 | Luke 20:27-47 | Ps. 75:8-10 |
| 3-May | Judg. 15-16 | Luke 21:1-19 | Ps. 76:1-7 |
| 4-May | Judg. 17-18 | Luke 21:20-22:6 | Ps. 76:8-12 |
| 5-May | Judg. 19:1-20:23 | Luke 22:7-30 | Ps. 77:1-11 |
| 6-May | Judg. 20:24-21:25 | Luke 22:31-54 | Ps. 77:12-20 |
| 7-May | Ruth 1-2 | Luke 22:55-23:25 | Ps. 78:1-4 |
| 8-May | Ruth 3-4 | Luke 23:26-24:12 | Ps. 78:5-8 |
| 9-May | 1 Sam. 1:1-2:21 | Luke 24:13-53 | Ps. 78:9-16 |
| 10-May | 1 Sam. 2:22-4:22 | John 1:1-28 | Ps. 78:17-24 |
| 11-May | 1 Sam. 5-7 | John 1:29-51 | Ps. 78:25-33 |
| 12-May | 1 Sam. 8:1-9:26 | John 2 | Ps. 78:34-41 |
| 13-May | 1 Sam. 9:27-11:15 | John 3:1-22 | Ps. 78:42-55 |
| 14-May | 1 Sam. 12-13 | John 3:23-4:10 | Ps. 78:56-66 |

| | | |
|---|---|---|
| 15-May | 1 Sam. 14 | John 4:11-38 | Ps. 78:67-72 |
| 16-May | 1 Sam. 15-16 | John 4:39-54 | Ps. 79:1-7 |
| 17-May | 1 Sam. 17 | John 5:1-24 | Ps. 79:8-13 |
| 18-May | 1 Sam. 18-19 | John 5:25-47 | Ps. 80:1-7 |
| 19-May | 1 Sam. 20-21 | John 6:1-21 | Ps. 80:8-19 |
| 20-May | 1 Sam. 22-23 | John 6:22-42 | Ps. 81:1-10 |
| 21-May | 1 Sam. 24:1-25:31 | John 6:43-71 | Ps. 81:11-16 |
| 22-May | 1 Sam. 25:32-27:12 | John 7:1-24 | Ps. 82 |
| 23-May | 1 Sam. 28-29 | John 7:25-8:11 | Ps. 83 |
| 24-May | 1 Sam. 30-31 | John 8:12-47 | Ps. 84:1-4 |
| 25-May | 2 Sam. 1-2 | John 8:48-9:12 | Ps. 84:5-12 |
| 26-May | 2 Sam. 3-4 | John 9:13-34 | Ps. 85:1-7 |
| 27-May | 2 Sam. 5:1-7:17 | John 9:35-10:10 | Ps. 85:8-13 |
| 28-May | 2 Sam. 7:18-10:19 | John 10:11-30 | Ps. 86:1-10 |
| 29-May | 2 Sam. 11:1-12:25 | John 10:31-11:16 | Ps. 86:11-17 |
| 30-May | 2 Sam. 12:26-13:39 | John 11:17-54 | Ps. 87 |
| 31-May | 2 Sam. 14:1-15:12 | John 11:55-12:19 | Ps. 88:1-9 |
| 1-Jun | 2 Sam. 15:13-16:23 | John 12:20-43 | Ps. 88:10-18 |
| 2-Jun | 2 Sam. 17:1-18:18 | John 12:44-13:20 | Ps. 89:1-6 |
| 3-Jun | 2 Sam. 18:19-19:39 | John 13:21-38 | Ps. 89:7-13 |
| 4-Jun | 2 Sam. 19:40-21:22 | John 14:1-17 | Ps. 89:14-18 |
| 5-Jun | 2 Sam. 22:1-23:7 | John 14:18-15:27 | Ps. 89:19-29 |
| 6-Jun | 2 Sam. 23:8-24:25 | John 16:1-22 | Ps. 89:30-37 |
| 7-Jun | 1 Kings 1 | John 16:23-17:5 | Ps. 89:38-52 |
| 8-Jun | 1 Kings 2 | John 17:6-26 | Ps. 90:1-12 |
| 9-Jun | 1 Kings 3-4 | John 18:1-27 | Ps. 90:13-17 |
| 10-Jun | 1 Kings 5-6 | John 18:28-19:5 | Ps. 91:1-10 |
| 11-Jun | 1 Kings 7 | John 19:6-25a | Ps. 91:11-16 |
| 12-Jun | 1 Kings 8:1-53 | John 19:25b-42 | Ps. 92:1-9 |
| 13-Jun | 1 Kings 8:54-10:13 | John 20:1-18 | Ps. 92:10-15 |
| 14-Jun | 1 Kings 10:14-11:43 | John 20:19-31 | Ps. 93 |
| 15-Jun | 1 Kings 12:1-13:10 | John 21 | Ps. 94:1-11 |
| 16-Jun | 1 Kings 13:11-14:31 | Acts 1:1-11 | Ps. 94:12-23 |
| 17-Jun | 1 Kings 15:1-16:20 | Acts 1:12-26 | Ps. 95 |
| 18-Jun | 1 Kings 16:21-18:19 | Acts 2:1-21 | Ps. 96:1-8 |
| 19-Jun | 1 Kings 18:20-19:21 | Acts2:22-41 | Ps. 96:9-13 |
| 20-Jun | 1 Kings 20 | Acts 2:42-3:26 | Ps. 97:1-6 |
| 21-Jun | 1 Kings 21:1-22:28 | Acts 4:1-22 | Ps. 97:7-12 |
| 22-Jun | 1 Kings 22:29-<br>2 Kings 1:18 | Acts 4:23-5:11 | Ps. 98 |
| 23-Jun | 2 Kings 2-3 | Acts 5:12-28 | Ps. 99 |
| 24-Jun | 2 Kings 4 | Acts 5:29-6:15 | Ps. 100 |
| 25-Jun | 2 Kings 5:1-6:23 | Acts 7:1-16 | Ps. 101 |
| 26-Jun | 2 Kings 6:24-8:15 | Acts 7:17-36 | Ps. 102:1-7 |
| 27-Jun | 2 Kings 8:16-9:37 | Acts 7:37-53 | Ps. 102:8-17 |
| 28-Jun | 2 Kings 10-11 | Acts 7:54-8:8 | Ps. 102:18-28 |

| | | |
|---|---|---|
| 29-Jun | 2 Kings 12-13 | Acts 8:9-40 | Ps. 103:1-9 |
| 30-Jun | 2 Kings 14-15 | Acts 9:1-16 | Ps. 103:10-14 |
| 1-Jul | 2 Kings 16-17 | Acts 9:17-31 | Ps. 103:15-22 |
| 2-Jul | 2 Kings 18:1-19:7 | Acts 9:32-10:16 | Ps. 104:1-9 |
| 3-Jul | 2 Kings 19:8-20:21 | Acts 10:17-33 | Ps. 104:10-23 |
| 4-Jul | 2 Kings 21:1-22:20 | Acts 10:34-11:18 | Ps. 104: 24-30 |
| 5-Jul | 2 Kings 23 | Acts 11:19-12:17 | Ps. 104:31-35 |
| 6-Jul | 2 Kings 24-25 | Acts 12:18-13:13 | Ps. 105:1-7 |
| 7-Jul | 1 Chron. 1-2 | Acts 13:14-43 | Ps. 105:8-15 |
| 8-Jul | 1 Chron. 3:1-5:10 | Acts 13:44-14:10 | Ps. 105:16-28 |
| 9-Jul | 1 Chron. 5:11-6:81 | Acts 14:11-28 | Ps. 105:29-36 |
| 10-Jul | 1 Chron. 7:1-9:9 | Acts 15:1-18 | Ps. 105:37-45 |
| 11-Jul | 1 Chron. 9:10-11:9 | Acts 15:19-41 | Ps. 106:1-12 |
| 12-Jul | 1 Chron. 11:10-12:40 | Acts 16:1-15 | Ps. 106:13-27 |
| 13-Jul | 1 Chron. 13-15 | Acts 16:16-40 | Ps. 106:28-33 |
| 14-Jul | 1 Chron. 16-17 | Acts 17:1-14 | Ps. 106:34-43 |
| 15-Jul | 1 Chron. 18-20 | Acts 17:15-34 | Ps. 106:44-48 |
| 16-Jul | 1 Chron. 21-22 | Acts 18:1-23 | Ps. 107:1-9 |
| 17-Jul | 1 Chron. 23-25 | Acts 18:24-19:10 | Ps. 107:10-16 |
| 18-Jul | 1 Chron. 26-27 | Acts 19:11-22 | Ps. 107:17-32 |
| 19-Jul | 1 Chron. 28-29 | Acts 19:23-41 | Ps. 107:33-38 |
| 20-Jul | 2 Chron. 1-3 | Acts 20:1-16 | Ps. 107:39-43 |
| 21-Jul | 2 Chron. 4:1-6:11 | Acts 20:17-38 | Ps. 108 |
| 22-Jul | 2 Chron. 6:12-7:10 | Acts 21:1-14 | Ps. 109:1-20 |
| 23-Jul | 2 Chron. 7:11-9:28 | Acts 21:15-32 | Ps. 109:21-31 |
| 24-Jul | 2 Chron. 9:29-12:16 | Acts 21:33-22:16 | Ps. 110:1-3 |
| 25-Jul | 2 Chron. 13-15 | Acts 22:17-23:11 | Ps. 110:4-7 |
| 26-Jul | 2 Chron. 16-17 | Acts 23:12-24:21 | Ps. 111 |
| 27-Jul | 2 Chron. 18-19 | Acts 24:22-25:12 | Ps. 112 |
| 28-Jul | 2 Chron. 20-21 | Acts 25:13-27 | Ps. 113 |
| 29-Jul | 2 Chron. 22-23 | Acts 26 | Ps. 114 |
| 30-Jul | 2 Chron. 24:1-25:16 | Acts 27:1-20 | Ps. 115:1-10 |
| 31-Jul | 2 Chron. 25:17-27:9 | Acts 27:21-28:6 | Ps. 115:11-18 |
| 1-Aug | 2 Chron. 28:1-29:19 | Acts 28:7-31 | Ps. 116:1-5 |
| 2-Aug | 2 Chron. 29:20-30:27 | Rom. 1:1-17 | Ps. 116:6-19 |
| 3-Aug | 2 Chron. 31-32 | Rom. 1:18-32 | Ps. 117 |
| 4-Aug | 2 Chron. 33:1-34:7 | Rom. 2 | Ps. 118:1-18 |
| 5-Aug | 2 Chron. 34:8-35:19 | Rom. 3:1-26 | Ps. 118:19-23 |
| 6-Aug | 2 Chron. 35:20-36:23 | Rom. 3:27-4:25 | Ps. 118:24-29 |
| 7-Aug | Ezra 1-3 | Rom. 5 | Ps. 119:1-8 |
| 8-Aug | Ezra 4-5 | Rom. 6:1-7:6 | Ps. 119:9-16 |
| 9-Aug | Ezra 6:1-7:26 | Rom. 7:7-25 | Ps. 119:17-32 |
| 10-Aug | Ezra 7:27-9:4 | Rom. 8:1-27 | Ps. 119:33-40 |
| 11-Aug | Ezra 9:5-10:44 | Rom. 8:28-39 | Ps. 119:41-64 |
| 12-Aug | Neh. 1:1-3:16 | Rom. 9:1-18 | Ps. 119:65-72 |
| 13-Aug | Neh. 3:17-5:13 | Rom. 9:19-33 | Ps. 119:73-80 |

| | | |
|---|---|---|
| 14-Aug | Neh. 5:14-7:73 | Rom. 10:1-13 | Ps. 119:81-88 |
| 15-Aug | Neh. 8:1-9:5 | Rom. 10:14-11:24 | Ps. 119:89-104 |
| 16-Aug | Neh. 9:6-10:27 | Rom. 11:25-12:8 | Ps. 119:105-120 |
| 17-Aug | Neh. 10:28-12:26 | Rom. 12:9-13:7 | Ps. 119:121-128 |
| 18-Aug | Neh. 12:27-13:31 | Rom. 13:8-14:12 | Ps. 119:129-136 |
| 19-Aug | Esther 1:1-2:18 | Rom. 14:13-15:13 | Ps. 119:137-152 |
| 20-Aug | Esther 2:19-5:14 | Rom. 15:14-21 | Ps. 119:153-168 |
| 21-Aug | Esther. 6-8 | Rom. 15:22-33 | Ps. 119:169-176 |
| 22-Aug | Esther 9-10 | Rom. 16 | Ps. 120-122 |
| 23-Aug | Job 1-3 | 1 Cor. 1:1-25 | Ps. 123 |
| 24-Aug | Job 4-6 | 1 Cor. 1:26-2:16 | Ps. 124-125 |
| 25-Aug | Job 7-9 | 1 Cor. 3 | Ps. 126-127 |
| 26-Aug | Job 10-13 | 1 Cor. 4:1-13 | Ps. 128-129 |
| 27-Aug | Job 14-16 | 1 Cor. 4:14-5:13 | Ps. 130 |
| 28-Aug | Job 17-20 | 1 Cor. 6 | Ps. 131 |
| 29-Aug | Job 21-23 | 1 Cor. 7:1-16 | Ps. 132 |
| 30-Aug | Job 24-27 | 1 Cor. 7:17-40 | Ps. 133-134 |
| 31-Aug | Job 28-30 | 1 Cor. 8 | Ps. 135 |
| 1-Sep | Job 31-33 | 1 Cor. 9:1-18 | Ps. 136:1-9 |
| 2-Sep | Job 34-36 | 1 Cor. 9:19-10:13 | Ps. 136:10-26 |
| 3-Sep | Job 37-39 | 1 Cor. 10:14-11:1 | Ps. 137 |
| 4-Sep | Job 40-42 | 1 Cor. 11:2-34 | Ps. 138 |
| 5-Sep | Eccles. 1:1-3:15 | 1 Cor. 12:1-26 | Ps. 139:1-6 |
| 6-Sep | Eccles. 3:16-6:12 | 1 Cor. 12:27-13:13 | Ps. 139:7-18 |
| 7-Sep | Eccles. 7:1-9:12 | 1 Cor. 14:1-22 | Ps. 139:19-24 |
| 8-Sep | Eccles. 9:13-12:14 | 1 Cor. 14:23-15:11 | Ps. 140:1-8 |
| 9-Sep | SS 1-4 | 1 Cor. 15:12-34 | Ps. 140:9-13 |
| 10-Sep | SS 5-8 | 1 Cor. 15:35-58 | Ps. 141 |
| 11-Sep | Isa. 1-2 | 1 Cor. 16 | Ps. 142 |
| 12-Sep | Isa. 3-5 | 2 Cor. 1:1-11 | Ps. 143:1-6 |
| 13-Sep | Isa. 6-8 | 2 Cor. 1:12-2:4 | Ps. 143:7-12 |
| 14-Sep | Isa. 9-10 | 2 Cor. 2:5-17 | Ps. 144 |
| 15-Sep | Isa. 11-13 | 2 Cor. 3 | Ps. 145 |
| 16-Sep | Isa. 14-16 | 2 Cor. 4 | Ps. 146 |
| 17-Sep | Isa. 17-19 | 2 Cor. 5 | Ps. 147:1-11 |
| 18-Sep | Isa. 20-23 | 2 Cor. 6 | Ps. 147:12-20 |
| 19-Sep | Isa. 24:1-26:19 | 2 Cor. 7 | Ps. 148 |
| 20-Sep | Isa. 26:20-28:29 | 2 Cor. 8 | Ps. 149-150 |
| 21-Sep | Isa. 29-30 | 2 Cor. 9 | Prov. 1:1-9 |
| 22-Sep | Isa. 31-33 | 2 Cor. 10 | Prov. 1:10-22 |
| 23-Sep | Isa. 34-36 | 2 Cor. 11 | Prov. 1:23-26 |
| 24-Sep | Isa. 37-38 | 2 Cor. 12:1-10 | Prov. 1:27-33 |
| 25-Sep | Isa. 39-40 | 2 Cor. 12:11-13:14 | Prov. 2:1-15 |
| 26-Sep | Isa. 41-42 | Gal. 1 | Prov. 2:16-22 |
| 27-Sep | Isa. 43:1-44:20 | Gal. 2 | Prov. 3:1-12 |
| 28-Sep | Isa. 44:21-46:13 | Gal. 3:1-18 | Prov. 3:13-26 |

| | | | |
|---|---|---|---|
| 29-Sep | Isa. 47:1-49:13 | Gal 3:19-29 | Prov. 3:27-35 |
| 30-Sep | Isa. 49:14-51:23 | Gal 4:1-11 | Prov. 4:1-19 |
| 1-Oct | Isa. 52-54 | Gal. 4:12-31 | Prov. 4:20-27 |
| 2-Oct | Isa. 55-57 | Gal. 5 | Prov. 5:1-14 |
| 3-Oct | Isa. 58-59 | Gal. 6 | Prov. 5:15-23 |
| 4-Oct | Isa. 60-62 | Eph. 1 | Prov. 6:1-5 |
| 5-Oct | Isa. 63:1-65:16 | Eph. 2 | Prov. 6:6-19 |
| 6-Oct | Isa. 65:17-66:24 | Eph. 3:1-4:16 | Prov. 6:20-26 |
| 7-Oct | Jer. 1-2 | Eph. 4:17-32 | Prov. 6:27-35 |
| 8-Oct | Jer. 3:1-4:22 | Eph. 5 | Prov. 7:1-5 |
| 9-Oct | Jer. 4:23-5:31 | Eph. 6 | Prov. 7:6-27 |
| 10-Oct | Jer. 6:1-7:26 | Phil. 1:1-26 | Prov. 8:1-11 |
| 11-Oct | Jer. 7:26-9:16 | Phil. 1:27-2:18 | Prov. 8:12-21 |
| 12-Oct | Jer. 9:17-11:17 | Phil 2:19-30 | Prov. 8:22-36 |
| 13-Oct | Jer. 11:18-13:27 | Phil. 3 | Prov. 9:1-6 |
| 14-Oct | Jer. 14-15 | Phil. 4 | Prov. 9:7-18 |
| 15-Oct | Jer. 16-17 | Col. 1:1-23 | Prov. 10:1-5 |
| 16-Oct | Jer. 18:1-20:6 | Col. 1:24-2:15 | Prov. 10:6-14 |
| 17-Oct | Jer. 20:7-22:19 | Col. 2:16-3:4 | Prov. 10:15-26 |
| 18-Oct | Jer. 22:20-23:40 | Col. 3:5-4:1 | Prov. 10:27-32 |
| 19-Oct | Jer. 24-25 | Col. 4:2-18 | Prov. 11:1-11 |
| 20-Oct | Jer. 26-27 | 1 Thes. 1:1-2:8 | Prov. 11:12-21 |
| 21-Oct | Jer. 28-29 | 1 Thes. 2:9-3:13 | Prov. 11:22-26 |
| 22-Oct | Jer. 30:1-31:22 | 1 Thes. 4:1-5:11 | Prov. 11:27-31 |
| 23-Oct | Jer. 31:23-32:35 | 1 Thes. 5:12-28 | Prov. 12:1-14 |
| 24-Oct | Jer. 32:36-34:7 | 2 Thes. 1-2 | Prov. 12:15-20 |
| 25-Oct | Jer. 34:8-36:10 | 2 Thes. 3 | Prov. 12:21-28 |
| 26-Oct | Jer. 36:11-38:13 | 1 Tim. 1:1-17 | Prov. 13:1-4 |
| 27-Oct | Jer. 38:14-40:6 | 1 Tim. 1:18-3:13 | Prov. 13:5-13 |
| 28-Oct | Jer. 40:7-42:22 | 1 Tim. 3:14-4:10 | Prov. 13:14-21 |
| 29-Oct | Jer. 43-44 | 1 Tim. 4:11-5:16 | Prov. 13:22-25 |
| 30-Oct | Jer. 45-47 | 1 Tim. 5:17-6:21 | Prov. 14:1-6 |
| 31-Oct | Jer. 48:1-49:6 | 2 Tim. 1 | Prov. 14:7-22 |
| 1-Nov | Jer. 49:7-50:16 | 2 Tim. 2 | Prov. 14:23-27 |
| 2-Nov | Jer. 50:17-51:14 | 2 Tim. 3 | Prov. 14:28-35 |
| 3-Nov | Jer. 51:15-64 | 2 Tim. 4 | Prov. 15:1-9 |
| 4-Nov | Jer. 52-Lam. 1 | Ti. 1:1-9 | Prov. 15:10-17 |
| 5-Nov | Lam. 2:1-3:38 | Ti. 1:10-2:15 | Prov. 15:18-26 |
| 6-Nov | Lam. 3:39-5:22 | Ti. 3 | Prov. 15:27-33 |
| 7-Nov | Ezek. 1:1-3:21 | Philemon 1 | Prov. 16:1-9 |
| 8-Nov | Ezek. 3:22-5:17 | Heb. 1:1-2:4 | Prov. 16:10-21 |
| 9-Nov | Ezek. 6-7 | Heb. 2:5-18 | Prov. 16:22-33 |
| 10-Nov | Ezek. 8-10 | Heb. 3:1-4:3 | Prov. 17:1-5 |
| 11-Nov | Ezek. 11-12 | Heb. 4:4-5:10 | Prov. 17:6-12 |
| 12-Nov | Ezek. 13-14 | Heb. 5:11-6:20 | Prov. 17:13-22 |
| 13-Nov | Ezek. 15:1-16:43 | Heb. 7:1-28 | Prov. 17:23-28 |

| | | |
|---|---|---|
| 14-Nov | Ezek. 16:44-17:24 | Heb. 8:1-9:10 | Prov. 18:1-7 |
| 15-Nov | Ezek. 18-19 | Heb. 9:11-28 | Prov. 18:8-17 |
| 16-Nov | Ezek. 20 | Heb. 10:1-25 | Prov. 18:18-24 |
| 17-Nov | Ezek. 21-22 | Heb. 10:26-39 | Prov. 19:1-8 |
| 18-Nov | Ezek. 23 | Heb. 11:1-31 | Prov. 19:9-14 |
| 19-Nov | Ezek. 24-26 | Heb. 11:32-40 | Prov. 19:15-21 |
| 20-Nov | Ezek. 27-28 | Heb. 12:1-13 | Prov. 19:22-29 |
| 21-Nov | Ezek. 29-30 | Heb. 12:14-29 | Prov. 20:1-18 |
| 22-Nov | Ezek. 31-32 | Heb. 13 | Prov. 20:19-24 |
| 23-Nov | Ezek. 33:1-34:10 | Jas. 1 | Prov. 20:25-30 |
| 24-Nov | Ezek. 34:11-36:15 | Jas. 2 | Prov. 21:1-8 |
| 25-Nov | Ezek. 36:16-37:28 | Jas. 3 | Prov. 21:9-18 |
| 26-Nov | Ezek. 38-39 | Jas. 4:1-5:6 | Prov. 21:19-24 |
| 27-Nov | Ezek. 40 | Jas. 5:7-20 | Prov. 21:25-31 |
| 28-Nov | Ezek. 41:1-43:12 | 1 Pet. 1:1-12 | Prov. 22:1-9 |
| 29-Nov | Ezek. 43:13-44:31 | 1 Pet. 1:13-2:3 | Prov. 22:10-23 |
| 30-Nov | Ezek. 45-46 | 1 Pet. 2:4-17 | Prov. 22:24-29 |
| 1-Dec | Ezek. 47-48 | 1 Pet. 2:18-3:7 | Prov. 23:1-9 |
| 2-Dec | Dan. 1:1-2:23 | 1 Pet. 3:8-4:19 | Prov. 23:10-16 |
| 3-Dec | Dan. 2:24-3:30 | 1 Pet. 5 | Prov. 23:17-25 |
| 4-Dec | Dan. 4 | 2 Pet. 1 | Prov. 23:26-35 |
| 5-Dec | Dan. 5 | 2 Pet. 2 | Prov. 24:1-18 |
| 6-Dec | Dan. 6:1-7:14 | 2 Pet. 3 | Prov. 24:19-27 |
| 7-Dec | Dan. 7:15-8:27 | 1 John 1:1-2:17 | Prov. 24:28-34 |
| 8-Dec | Dan. 9-10 | 1 John 2:18-29 | Prov. 25:1-12 |
| 9-Dec | Dan. 11-12 | 1 John 3:1-12 | Prov. 25:13-17 |
| 10-Dec | Hos. 1-3 | 1 John 3:13-4:16 | Prov. 25:18-28 |
| 11-Dec | Hos. 4-6 | 1 John 4:17-5:21 | Prov. 26:1-16 |
| 12-Dec | Hos. 7-10 | 2 John | Prov. 26:17-21 |
| 13-Dec | Hos. 11-14 | 3 John | Prov. 26:22-27:9 |
| 14-Dec | Joel 1:1-2:17 | Jude | Prov. 27:10-17 |
| 15-Dec | Joel 2:18-3:21 | Rev. 1:1-2:11 | Prov. 27:18-27 |
| 16-Dec | Amos 1:1-4:5 | Rev. 2:12-29 | Prov. 28:1-8 |
| 17-Dec | Amos 4:6-6:14 | Rev. 3 | Prov. 28:9-16 |
| 18-Dec | Amos 7-9 | Rev. 4:1-5:5 | Prov. 28:17-24 |
| 19-Dec | Obad-Jonah | Rev. 5:6-14 | Prov. 28:25-28 |
| 20-Dec | Mic. 1:1-4:5 | Rev. 6:1-7:8 | Prov. 29:1-8 |
| 21-Dec | Mic. 4:6-7:20 | Rev. 7:9-8:13 | Prov. 29:9-14 |
| 22-Dec | Nah. 1-3 | Rev. 9-10 | Prov. 29:15-23 |
| 23-Dec | Hab. 1-3 | Rev. 11 | Prov. 29:24-27 |
| 24-Dec | Zeph. 1-3 | Rev. 12 | Prov. 30:1-6 |
| 25-Dec | Hag. 1-2 | Rev. 13:1-14:13 | Prov. 30:7-16 |
| 26-Dec | Zech. 1-4 | Rev. 14:14-16:3 | Prov. 30:17-20 |
| 27-Dec | Zech. 5-8 | Rev. 16:4-21 | Prov. 30:21-28 |
| 28-Dec | Zech. 9-11 | Rev. 17:1-18:8 | Prov. 30:29-33 |
| 29-Dec | Zech. 12-14 | Rev. 18:9-24 | Prov. 31:1-9 |
| 30-Dec | Mal. 1-2 | Rev. 19-20 | Prov. 31:10-17 |
| 31-Dec | Mal. 3-4 | Rev. 21-22 | Prov. 31:18-31 |